UNOFFICIAL MAKERS OF PUBLIC POLICY
PEOPLE AND PARTIES IN POLITICS

JOHN H. FENTON
University of Massachusetts

with an introduction by
EARLE C. CLEMENTS

SCOTT, FORESMAN AMERICAN GOVERNMENT SERIES
Joseph C. Palamountain, Jr., Editor

SCOTT, FORESMAN AND COMPANY

To Eve

ACKNOWLEDGMENTS

It is appropriate to begin my study of American politics by paying tribute to the late Professor V. O. Key, Jr., of Harvard University, whose books, lectures, and guidance of my Ph.D. dissertation combined to provide me with a useful map of the political world.

I am grateful to many people for their direct help in the research and writing of this book. Mr. Alan Merdek and others at the University of Massachusetts Computer Center provided invaluable assistance in my efforts to use the computer. The editor of the Scott, Foresman American Government Series, Joseph C. Palamountain, Jr., was more than routinely helpful; his observations and criticisms were thought-provoking and stimulating and contributed a great deal to whatever excellence may be found in the final product. I am grateful to Mrs. Sharon Baumgartner for her help in preparing the manuscript for publication. Mrs. Doris Holden, my typist, deserves many thanks for the Saturdays and Sundays she sacrificed in order to help me meet publisher's deadlines. Finally, I am grateful to my wife Peake, my daughter Margaret, and my son Johnny for their tolerance of a busy and distracted husband and father.

JOHN H. FENTON

The symbol on the cover consists of details from cartoons by Thomas Nast.
The Republican elephant (1874) is used by permission of Brown Brothers.
The Democratic donkey (1870) is used by permission of Culver Pictures, Inc.

Library of Congress Catalog Card No. 66-20348 6170
Copyright © 1966 by Scott, Foresman and Company, Glenview, Illinois 60025
All rights reserved. Printed in the United States of America
Regional offices of Scott, Foresman and Company are located in Atlanta,
Dallas, Glenview, Palo Alto, and Oakland, N.J.

PREFACE

The American System of government strikes a balance between unity and diversity. There is a unity to our system, but it is a unity which tolerates—indeed, requires for its vigor and viability—a broad diversity of institutions, processes, and participants. By organizing the analysis of the sprawling complexity of the American system into smaller, coherent, but interlocking units, the Scott, Foresman American Government Series attempts to reflect this pluralistic balance.

This approach, we believe, has several important advantages over the usual one-volume presentation of analytical and descriptive material. By giving the reader more manageable units, and by introducing him to the underlying and unifying strands of those units, it puts him in a better position to comprehend both the whole and its components. It should enable him to avoid the not-uncommon circumstance of viewing the American system as a morass of interminable and unconnected facts and descriptions.

This approach certainly permits us to tap the expertise and experience of distinguished scholars in the fields of their special competence. Each writes about his specialties, and none is forced to deal with subjects remote from his ken or heart for the sake of "completeness." The unity of the series rests on the interlocking of the various volumes and, in the general emphasis on policy and policy-making, on the method of analysis as opposed to simple description. It does not rest on a unity of approach. The authors vary in their values, their accents, and the questions they ask. To have attempted to impose unity in these matters would have been to water down the series, for the diversity of approach reflects the diversity of the system, its participants, and its commentators. But the final value of this series and its ultimate balance between unity and diversity rest, of course, in the use to which it is put by the reader.

Politics is the art of the possible, and in this volume John Fenton has stressed the realities of politics, while not ignoring the more theoretical and idealistic dimensions of the subject. His discussion is enriched by his familiarity with the broad range of political systems to be found in the United States. The resultant blend is one which should well prepare the reader to understand, to evaluate, and to participate.

Joseph C. Palamountain, Jr., *Editor*

INTRODUCTION

I am not in the least unmindful of the proper role of the writer of a preface, but as a practical politician I find it difficult to cast aside the tendency to criticize efforts of the scholarly world to view the political actions of men within the confines of the test tube. To say at the outset that I have some reservations about the author's "facts," as well as about some of his conclusions, will in part fulfill my new role as a "preface writer" as well as maintain my perspective as a politician, for I have no doubt that my disagreement with the author on some points will make the text all the more appealing to many readers.

Not since the birth of our democracy have political theoreticians and political scientists been sufficiently free from disruption and distraction by history-shaking events to evaluate the political structure of our nation and people. Yet research and thought are the processes by which progress is made. There is some danger that the excitement of research in space and other technological investigations will attract the young Jeffersons and Hamiltons of our day into scientific pursuits, leaving political and social studies to the less imaginative. I hope not. For now, perhaps more than at any other time, the growth of our democracy, the translation of new technology into proper uses by a free people, and the relationship of our nation to others in a shrunken world demand precise research, the best thought, and, of course, prudent action. Yet, in spite of the urgent need, far too little research is undertaken in the political and social fields, and far too little effort goes into the collection of data to feed the political researchers. Our census is still a decennial affair, even though population growths and moves and technological changes in ten years are now comparable to those in a hundred-year period in the earlier history of our nation and to those in a thousand-year period in the earlier history of civilization. The data skillfully employed in this text to measure "state effort" is widely recognized as acceptable for that purpose—acceptable because it is the only data available which has been uniformly collected for all the states. Yet it is based solely on personal income and does not reflect other indices of a state's financial resources (i.e., corporate income and wealth, property valuations), which, if available in addition to personal income data, would be a more accurate measure of a state's financial ability.

The reader will be impressed with the scientific manner in which the author approaches his subject in the first pages—is it true that "issue-oriented" two-party politics is superior to "job-oriented" two-party politics? At the same time, as is the case with all useful and timed research, the careful reader will find points that invite further investigation and analysis. Moreover, the reader will be challenged to separate proven fact from persuasive rationalization. The author is extremely gifted in this latter regard and is able to bring the reader breathless to a number of conclusions to which less artful writers would not have ventured. The text warns that the recent Democratic election victories may prove Pyrrhic for the Democratic party—a conviction that I certainly do not share but find extremely interesting and challenging. In short, the final pages of the treatise seem to call upon the author for another work, which I, for one, hope will be forthcoming. The final chapter also, I feel confident, will invite other scholars to further research and study of the nature and composition of American political parties.

EARLE C. CLEMENTS

TABLE OF CONTENTS

PREFACE iii

INTRODUCTION iv

CHAPTER ONE ★ THE STUDY OF AMERICAN POLITICAL PARTIES . . 1
A Brief History of the Two-Party System
Party Competition and Leadership
Parties and Interest Groups
Party Organization
Relationship of Parties and National Government
Approaches to the Study of Political Parties
Conclusions

CHAPTER TWO ★ TWO-PARTY COMPETITION:
DOES IT MAKE A DIFFERENCE? 31
Differential Intensity of Competition
Effects of Competition and Other Variables on Government
    Performance
Conclusions

CHAPTER THREE ★ TWO-PARTY ISSUE-ORIENTED POLITICS 50
Emergence of Issue-Oriented Parties
Process of Political Transformation
Characteristics and Goals
Relationship to Public Opinion
Relationship to Interest Groups
Effect on Government Performance
Conclusions

CHAPTER FOUR ★ TWO-PARTY JOB-ORIENTED POLITICS 66
Job-Oriented Politics in Kentucky
Relationship to Public Opinion
Relationship to Interest Groups
Effect on Government Performance
Conclusions

CHAPTER FIVE ★ ONE-PARTY POLITICS 78
Causes of One-Party Politics
Multifactional One-Party Politics
Bifactional One-Party Politics
Effect on Government Performance

CHAPTER SIX ★ NATIONAL TWO-PARTY POLITICS 90
National Party Organizations
Causes of Party Nationalization
Summary

CHAPTER SEVEN ★ THE AMERICAN POLITICAL FUTURE 108
Isolation vs. Community
The 1964 Presidential Campaign
Political Trends in the Midwest
Political Trends in the Cities
Political Trends in the Nation

FOOTNOTES 133

BIBLIOGRAPHICAL ESSAY 138

INDEX 144

The Study of American Political Parties

Competition between two political parties in periodic elections is the way citizens of the United States solve the "Who shall rule?" problem. The two-party competition formula for determining the identity of Presidents and congressmen, governors and state legislators, has served Americans reasonably satisfactorily over most of the life of the nation. Certainly the American rulers selected thereby compare favorably in terms of performance on the job with the kings or commissars of nations that use other methods of determining the identity of their chiefs of state.

The student of American political parties wants information concerning the origins and operations of the American competitive political system — i.e., where did the parties come from and how do they work? Students of political parties are also concerned with changes that are taking place in the operations of the political parties and with possible improvements that might be introduced into their organization and functions to enable them to better serve the nation. Our first concern, then, is the origins of political parties; second, broad theories of how the American two-party system functions; third, an examination of the ways in which the parties actually work in the 1960's and the "pay-offs" of their operation; and, finally, the directions being taken by American political parties.

A BRIEF HISTORY OF THE TWO-PARTY SYSTEM

ORIGINS

The political party has its roots in the omnipresent struggle for power within and between human communities. As far back as man can remember, chiefs, princes, tyrants, and presidents have ruled his tribes and cities and nations. The rationalization for the existence of governments has usually been the necessity to provide for the common defense of the community and to insure its domestic tranquillity. Man's written history shows, too, that the chieftains and princes and tyrants have had to be perpetually on guard against individuals and groups plotting to seize their positions and their power under one pretext or another. The ancient palace struggles between the "ins" and the "outs" were political party battles in their most primitive form.

The American two-party competitive political system is far removed from such primitive beginnings. However, in the early days of the nation the first stirrings of two-party political competition bore certain similarities to the earlier forms of political combat. The political life of eighteenth-century United States was dominated by the Washingtons and Jeffersons (i.e., the rural gentry) and the Hamiltons and Adamses (i.e., the Eastern financial and mercantile leaders). However, the rural and financial gentry were not of one mind on public policy issues, and they were also divided over the identity of the individuals who should rule the nation. In part, the division of the gentry was inherited from England, where the Whigs and Tories contested control of public office. A second cause was the infection of a part of the gentry, such as Thomas Jefferson, with democratic ideology. A third cause of division among the gentry was clashing ambition and desire for power on the part of individuals such as Alexander Hamilton, Aaron Burr, and Jefferson.

The two-party form probably had its roots in the English political system from which the Americans derived most of their political values. Two features of British politics were especially important: a rough two-party system and the custom of settling political disputes between the gentry and the financial and mercantile interests through elections. The founders of the United

States incorporated elections into the Constitution, and the custom of dividing into two competitive political parties gave the voters candidates and issues to choose between. The democratizing experiences of the frontier were another important factor in the development of a two-party system. The pioneers discovered that energy, initiative, and cooperative efforts enabled them to clear fields of forests, build homes, and provide security from Indians, and that class distinctions were rather useless and, in fact, dysfunctional in securing these ends. It was these frontier experiences that gave substantive meaning to the liberal ideas of Thomas Paine, Thomas Jefferson, and Andrew Jackson. It was in these communities that the notion that one man was as good as another took solid root. And from these experiences and ideas there was generated the demand for universal suffrage that made the United States a democracy.

The reason for the persistence of a two-party competitive politics in the United States is a favorite topic for conjecture by political scientists, but probably no single cause can be found. Any list of causes must include the Whig vs. Tory tradition, brought to the New World from England, as well as the nature of the political divisions that first split the citizens of the United States into only two major factions: those for and those against the Constitution. Subsequent political divisions also tended to take a two-sided form: the Western frontiersmen vs. the Eastern merchants and bankers, the North vs. the South, the more well-to-do vs. the less well-to-do. The absence of multiple divisions leading to a multiparty system might be attributed to the essential homogeneity of the population in terms of values, ideology, experience, ethnic background, and religion. A true community of interests, backed by shared values, prevented the splitting of the nation into numberless warring political sects.

A final factor contributing to the maintenance of a two-party system in the United States is the method of electing most senators, representatives, and executives at both state and national levels by a plurality vote in single-member districts. Therefore, if a third party splits from one of the two major parties, it has little chance of electing any of its candidates to office. However, if there were a system of election by proportional representation in multimember districts, then the third party would receive representation in the halls of Congress and in the state legislatures roughly in proportion to the vote received. The theory goes that potential schisms are frequently warded off by the fact that under American electoral practice political party rebels almost certainly face total electoral defeat when they form a third party. Therefore, the rebels reconcile themselves to an undesirable situation and accept the half a loaf they may be offered by the major party rather than tilt with windmills in pursuit of the entire loaf.

In summary, the character of the two-party division in the United States has been the product of, first, major events; second, the reactions to the events of the political parties and their candidates; and third, the impact on the voters of both the events and the reactions of parties and politicians to the events. The following brief summary of major events and their impact on the parties and the electorate is designed to provide an understanding of the causative agents behind the two-party political system as it operates in the United States in the 1960's.[1]

PARTY AFFILIATION

At base, the two-party, competitive, political form in the United States is a product of the tendency of most Americans to identify with, or regard themselves as members of, one of the two major political parties. The parties derive their strength as well as their distinctive policy positions from the qualitative differences in their mass memberships. Although there are high-income Democrats as well as Republicans and laboring-class Republicans as well as Democrats, the Democratic party in the United States tends to be the political home of the less well-to-do members of the citizenry, while the Republican party generally houses the more well-to-do. In addition, most Catholics, Negroes, Americans of Irish and Eastern European descent, and people residing in the Southern United States and in the cities of the North identify their interests with the Democratic party, whereas most Republican voters are to be found on the other side of the sociological coin—that is, among native white Protestants, Americans of Western European descent, and residents of less urban and suburban areas of both the North and the South.

The causative factors behind the identification of most Americans with one political party or another may be found in one or more of the major political events in the history of the nation and the effect of the event upon them as individuals or upon their forebears. The first important event that fixed the political loyalties of Americans was the "Age of Jackson." Jackson campaigned as the champion of the "common man" in the elections of 1824, 1828, and 1832. The bitter political battles between the Democratic party, headed by Jackson, and the more conservative Whig party and its candidates resulted in a division of Americans between the two parties along both sectional and economic lines. The Western frontiersmen often owed the Eastern bankers money and therefore responded positively to Jackson's attacks upon the Eastern financiers. The citizens of the Eastern United States, and particularly the financial and mercantile communities concentrated there, found less to cheer about in Jackson's attacks upon the moneyed interests. To some degree, at least, the identification of the Democratic party in the minds of some Americans with the welfare of the common man is traceable to the Jacksonian period of American history. In some sections of the nation, such as certain counties in eastern and western Kentucky, the Democratic predilection of a majority of the voters dates from the 1828 election and continues untarnished by so much as a single Whig or Republican victory through the 1964 Democratic landslide.

The second major event that helped determine the political preferences of Americans was the Civil War. The issues of the Civil War cut across economic lines and tended to push Northerners, both rich and poor, into the Republican party and white Southerners, including sharecroppers, yeomen farmers, and plantation owners, into the Democratic party. However, those who had moved from the South into states such as Ohio, Indiana, and Illinois before 1860 found themselves torn between loyalty to the Union and sympathy with their Southern cousins. Many such transplanted Southerners found the Democratic party a comfortable political home because of its identification with the goal of a negotiated settlement of the war. The Northerners of Southern ancestry who were antipathetic to the Civil War were called Copperheads and suffered from much persecution during the civil strife.

Similarly, there were low-income white people, residing primarily in the mountainous areas of the South, who owned no slaves and were pro-Union. These Southern sympathizers with the Northern cause became some of the more loyal Republican voters in the nation as a consequence of the events of the 1860's. However, the fact that the mountain Republicans were a small minority and that there were few people of Northern ancestry living in the South at the time of the Civil War accounts in part for the one-party system that developed thereafter.

Finally, the Negroes of both the North and the South voted Republican after the Civil War out of gratitude for Abraham Lincoln's Emancipation Proclamation. Thus, in the South the slave-owners became Democrats and the former slaves voted Republican after 1865. The result would have been a standoff, in terms of votes, if the white Southerners had not deprived the Negro of the ballot in the latter part of the nineteenth century. But by virtue of the disenfranchisement of the Negro, the South became a bulwark of national Democratic voting strength from shortly after the Civil War until the candidacy of Republican Barry Goldwater in 1964.

In the 1960's the lingering effect of the Civil War upon party affiliations of the citizenry could still be observed in scores of states. The sections of Maryland, Missouri, Kentucky, and West Virginia where there had been slavery before the Civil War, and the sections of Indiana and Illinois that were settled by Southerners, tended in the 1960's to remain Democratic strongholds. Examples of these Civil War-based Democratic strongholds in the 1960's included the Little Dixie section of Missouri, the Pennroyal in Kentucky, the eastern shore of Maryland, the Greenbrier Plateau of West Virginia, the Little Egypt section of Illinois, and the river valleys of southern Indiana. On the Republican side, the sections of Ohio, Indiana, and Illinois that had been settled by New Englanders and that were abolitionist strongholds before the Civil War, and the mountainous areas of Kentucky, Missouri, and Maryland where there had been no slaves, tended to remain the most Republican inclined of all the areas of their states. Examples of Republican inclined mountain areas included the western Ozarks of Missouri, the eastern and western Kentucky hills and mountains, and western Maryland. Examples of sections that were settled by abolitionist-inclined New Englanders and that remained Republican strongholds in the 1960's include the Ohio Land Company section of Ohio and the less urban portions of northern Illinois and Indiana.

A third important political event that influenced the political allegiance of Americans was the 1896 competition for the presidency between William Jennings Bryan, for the Democrats, and William McKinley, the Republican candidate. This presidential election climaxed a decade or more of political protest by the smaller farmers and small businessmen against the growth of business monopoly and the consequent tendency of railroads to charge whatever the traffic would bear for hauling the farmers' produce to market and for shipping goods to the small businessmen. Similarly, the small farmers and businessmen complained bitterly about the interest rates charged by Eastern bankers for mortgages on their farms and business establishments.

In 1896 William Jennings Bryan and the Democratic party proposed to lighten the burden of the little man through inflation, thus making it easier for him to pay his debts. The long-run significance of the 1896 election was that it helped push Americans back toward a political division along economic lines rather than along the sectional lines laid down by the Civil War. The candidacy in 1912 of Woodrow Wilson, a Progressive Democrat, and his subsequent actions as President also tended to give renewed life to the myth associating the Democratic party with the aspirations of the common man. Another effect of the Wilson administration was that Germans, many of whom were adherents of the Democratic political faith, were pushed into the Republican party as a result of America's entrance into World War I and the associated indignities suffered by Americans of German ancestry. The coincidence of Democratic Presidents holding office at the time of two great wars with Germany—1917 and 1941—had made confirmed Republicans of a majority of people of German ancestry in states such as Wisconsin, Minnesota, Ohio, and Missouri in the 1960's.

The fourth great event that shaped the membership and nature of the American two-party system was the Great Depression of 1929-1939. Unfortunately for the Republican party, its candidate for the presidency in 1928, Herbert Hoover, won the election and, consequently, was in office at the time of the stock market crash of 1929 and the subsequent hardship and unemployment that affected almost everyone in the nation. In 1932 a Democratic victory was virtually inevitable, and Franklin Roosevelt, the Democratic nominee, swept to a landslide victory over Hoover.

The first Roosevelt administration, 1933-1937, had a revolutionary impact upon American life and politics. Roosevelt and his administration asserted the doctrine that government has a positive role to play in assuring prosperity and employment through a wide variety of fiscal and monetary policies. Most important for the future of the two-party system, the measures adopted by the Roosevelt administration were primarily designed to help the less well-to-do in society. Management was forced to bargain collectively with labor unions through the National Labor Relations Act. Employers were forced to help provide for the security of their employees through the Social Security Act. Millions of dollars of tax funds were spent to provide jobs for the unemployed through the Works Progress and Public Works Administrations. Other New Deal legislation designed to reallocate goods and opportunities in the society or to regulate the use of wealth included the Agricultural Adjustment Act, the devaluation of the dollar (which helped debtors), the Home Owners Loan Corporation (which staved off foreclosures), the Securities Act, and the Tennessee Valley Authority. After the Roosevelt landslide of 1936 came passage of the Fair Labor Standards Act, which included provisions regulating the minimum wage employers could pay and the maximum hours they could work their employees.

The New Deal profoundly modified the sectional two-party division of the nation inherited from the Civil War by superimposing upon it a newly sharpened economic division of the electorate. In the 1936 election, the disadvantaged of the nation, including the traditionally Republican Negroes and the often-Republican workers in mass-production industries, cast their votes for Democrat Franklin Roosevelt in record numbers. At the same time, the more well-to-do of the nation voted one-sidedly in favor of the Republican candidate, Alfred Landon.

The 1936 election did not *introduce* an economic division of the electorate, for indeed it had never been absent after the national division over the Constitutional Convention of 1787. And even the sectional Civil War division of the nation was related to economics, for the South produced raw goods and the North was a manufacturing center. Further, after the Civil War the South was a center of poverty. Therefore, the criticisms of the economic system made by reformers always had a certain appeal for the people of the South of every class, for the South—not without reason—thought of itself as an exploited region. In addition, throughout the history of economic protest marked out by Jackson, Bryan, and Wilson, the Democratic party maintained a certain identification with the common man, particularly in the minds of less well-to-do farmers of the West, the border states, and the South.

In the cities of the North before 1932-1936, workers and employers had made common political cause in the Republican party. Workers in the steel mills and mines of Ohio, Kentucky, Indiana, and Illinois had joined hands with the Hannas, Harrimans, and Rockefellers in saving the nation from "bolshevism" through the election of William McKinley in 1896. The election of 1936 marked the close of this period of American political history when class divisions were minimized. After the 1936 presidential election, the core vote of the Democratic party consisted of these same working-class voters living in the great cities of the nation. The result was a new note of sharpness in the political dialogue between the candidates of the parties.

The final critical election to be discussed in this brief history of American two-party politics is the 1948 election, when Harry Truman beat off the challenge of Republican Thomas E. Dewey in spite of the defection of Democrats on the right, led by Strom Thurmond of South Carolina, and Democrats on the left, led by former Vice-President Henry A. Wallace. The 1948 election was important in shaping the nature of the American two-party system because of the civil rights issue, which split the Democratic party and thereby hastened the final blotting out of the sectional division of the parties and the nation brought on by the Civil War.

In the 1948 Democratic convention the liberals forced through a strong civil rights plank that conservative Southern elements in the party could not digest. As a consequence, Southern dissidents formed a Dixiecrat party and nominated Strom Thurmond of South Carolina as the party's presidential candidate and Fielding Wright of Mississippi as the vice-presidential candidate. The two Dixiecrat candidates carried four Southern states, where they supplanted Truman and Barkley as the "Democratic" party's candidates by virtue of decisions made by the states' Democratic parties. In Alabama, Truman and Barkley did not appear on the ballot.

The maximum objective of the Dixiecrats was to win enough states to deprive both Truman and Dewey of a majority of the electoral college vote and thereby throw the election into the House of Representatives, where Dixiecrats expected to play a pivotal role. It was hoped that the eleven states of the old Confederacy in combination with conservative delegations from other states could elect a conservative President. The minimum objective of the Dixiecrats was to frighten the national Democratic party into paying more attention to the demands of its Southern adherents.

The first or maximum hope of the Dixiecrats was not realized when Truman won a narrow electoral college majority. The second objective was approximated when, in the 1952 and 1956 Democratic conventions, the moderates "watered down" the civil rights plank and permitted the Southern delegations to retain their convention seats in spite of their refusal to swear loyalty to the party ticket.

The principal effect of the 1948 Southern revolt was to provide a bridge for Southern conservatives from their long-time loyalty to the Democratic party to a new affiliation with the Republican party. In 1948 few traditional Democrats of the Deep South could bring themselves to vote for a Republican. The political propaganda that had long associated the Republican party with carpetbaggers and Negro rule was too deeply fixed in the minds of Southern Democrats to make a Republican vote feasible. However, it was possible for them to vote for a Dixiecrat whose name appeared on the Democratic roster. After once departing from their Democratic voting tradition in 1948, it was then psychologically easier for many of the conservative Southern Democrats to vote for popular Republican Dwight D. Eisenhower in 1952. Finally, by 1964, the ancient Democratic-Republican cleavages marked out by the Civil War were all but erased when traditional Southern Democrats by the millions cast their votes for Barry Goldwater, a conservative Republican candidate. In the same election, the Democratic candidate, Lyndon Johnson, won the old abolitionist strongholds in New England by two-to-one majorities.

In summary, the net effect of traumatic events—the Age of Jackson, the Civil War, the campaign of 1896, the Great Depression, and the Southern revolt of 1948—and of the reaction of the parties and candidates to the events was that the Democratic party attracted most (but no longer almost all) Southerners, less well-to-do people of the cities and countryside, and disadvantaged groups of people, including the Negroes, first- and second-generation immigrant groups, Jews, Catholics, and Eastern European people generally, whereas the weight of Republican voting strength more and more came from the native stock, South as well as North. It was a division as ancient as disputes between tribes that control water and those that seek water. It was a political split that was related to the problems and aspirations of the people of the nation and thereby made American elections meaningful. It also held within it the seeds of conflict that might sever the slender bonds holding the American community together. However, there were important elements in the operation of the American two-party system that served to mute and modify the economic, religious, sectional, and racial conflicts of the nation. The nature and character of these moderating elements will be discussed at length in the following section dealing with the nature and functions of the American two-party system.[2]

PARTY COMPETITION AND LEADERSHIP

Accidents and events in the history of the nation induced a fairly equal division of the electorate between two political parties roughly along the lines of contemporary problems. The next requirement of a competitive two-party system is leadership that makes the parties distinct entities, competes at every level of government, advocates alternative approaches to the problems that concern the voters, and, if victorious, carries through after election with laws and administrative decisions designed to translate promises into governmental practice (or, if in the minority, harasses the majority with criticism and surveillance of their stewardship).

Experience with the two-party system indicates that the leadership of a political party is almost inevitably closely attuned to the aspirations of its bedrock following. Therefore, if the electorate is divided between the parties along the lines of contemporary problems, then the leadership will almost certainly be similarly divided. In point of fact, the Democratic and Republican leadership in the 1960's seemed to be *more* widely divided on a variety of economic and social issues than were the rank and file of the parties.

Therefore, the broad conditions for meaningful two-party competition existed in the United States in the 1960's. Both the electorate and the leadership were similarly divided along the lines of the problems that faced them. The parties offered alternative platforms and candidates for election to office. After election, the victorious candidates became public officers, both serving the nation and acting as agents of their parties, in which position they could be held accountable for their stewardship. The minority party searched for flaws, mistakes, venality, and omissions in the governing party's stewardship and attempted to create conditions under which it could displace the majority party in subsequent elections.

There are, however, many features of the American two-party competitive system that serve to moderate the intensity of the political conflict between the parties. First, the division of the electorate along the lines of contemporary problems is never as clear-cut as the statistics of party composition might lead the observer to believe. Most members of labor unions are Democrats, but many are Republican inclined. Most Negroes are Democrats, but some 30 per cent will vote Republican if given half a chance. Similarly, most Protestants are Republicans, but 40 per cent or more will vote Democratic if given a reason to do so. Therefore, the leadership of both parties must at least give lip service to the party's desire to minister to the needs of every group in the society. Successful Democratic aspirants for the presidency must profess a tender regard for the needs of the business community as well as for the policy ends of labor unions — or suffer the electoral consequences. The experience of Barry Goldwater in 1964 indicates that a serious aspirant for the presidency on the Republican ticket cannot afford to walk roughshod on the sensibilities of Negroes, Eastern Europeans, or people drawing social security.

A second moderating influence on the leadership of the two major political parties is the substantial number of citizens who do not identify with either party. A political party that seriously hopes to win election cannot forfeit their votes. This consideration also tends to draw the leadership of both parties closer to the political middle of the road.

A final moderating influence on two-party competition is the cultural and constitutional features of American society which serve as barriers to radical political innovation. The cultural aspects of American society that keep two-party competition within reasonable ideological bounds include broad consensuses concerning such fundamentals as adherence to the Constitution and commitment to the principle of private ownership of property and the capitalistic system. Further, Americans generally assume that political parties and their candidates exist to serve the general welfare as opposed to the narrower ends of particular groups in society, such as labor, business, or farmers. Therefore, a party must try to identify its programs with the welfare of all groups in the nation, including profits for businessmen, wages for workers, and profits for farmers, if it is to enjoy any chance of success.

A variety of American political and governmental customs and institutions serve to cushion the impact on society of two-party competition. Most of them can be subsumed under the category of "checks and balances." Some of the checks and balances are required by the Constitution, including the various means by which political power is fragmented into legislative, executive, and judicial branches of government and into federal and state governments, and the checks that each of the several depositories of political power have over the actions of other branches and agencies. Checks upon overly militant two-party competition have developed outside the Constitution, including the methods of electing legislatures, which virtually assure control of the legislature by a different constellation of groups from that controlling the executive and which frequently result in divided political control of those two branches of government at both the national and state levels.

V. O. Key describes these mitigating features of two-party competition as "dualism in a moving consensus."[3] The two parties are rather widely separated ideologically and in terms of the core support they receive. However, in order to win elections the leadership must seek the middle of the political road. Therefore, the leadership of a party that constitutes a minority disgruntled by the innovations of the majority must actually exert strenuous effort to persuade its adherents that, after all, the innovations are not completely bad and that good tactics, if not good sense, demand acceptance of them. The best example of this role of a minority party's leadership is the efforts of Wendell Willkie, Thomas E. Dewey, Dwight Eisenhower, Richard Nixon, and, more recently, William Scranton and George Romney to persuade the "bitter-end" Republicans that the New Deal is part of the American consensus. The disastrous consequences of Barry Goldwater's attacks on social security testify to the validity of their logic.

By way of summary, the American two-party system provides the electorate with meaningful alternatives among candidates and policies by virtue of the division of the electorate into two political groups roughly along the lines of the problems facing them and the emergence of a political leadership reflective of these differences. However, the party combat is kept within reasonable bounds by a wide variety of cultural and institutional features that make it incumbent upon the candidates and other leaders of both parties to gravitate toward the political middle and that also render it somewhat difficult for the victorious party to translate into law any of its more extreme policy ends.

PARTIES AND INTEREST GROUPS

In the American two-party system, each party is, in a sense, a coalition of a large number and wide variety of groups and individuals. The more effective and articulate of these groups are also represented by formal organizations that usually function outside the parties and are commonly referred to as *interest* or *pressure* groups. Therefore, it is impossible to describe, much less understand, the organization and functions of political parties without including the role of interest groups in the political process.

A group, as commonly understood, consists of a number of people who interact rather frequently on the basis of some shared interest. According to this definition we would not consider left-handed people as a group simply by virtue of their left-handedness, but a formal organization of left-handed baseball pitchers would be a recognizable group based on a shared interest. An interest group differs from other groups in that it generally emerges out of the common dissatisfaction of its members with some aspect of the world in which they live. For example, bird lovers may become unhappy over the gradual disappearance of their feathered friends and organize an interest group to combat the depredations of hunters and other despoilers of wildlife. Commonly, interest groups fighting for their particular causes find it expedient to request government help in combating their enemies. Thus, the bird lovers might seek legislation or administrative decisions outlawing or limiting the slaying of birds by hunters.

In a complex industrial society there are a bewildering number of individuals who are unhappy enough with some aspect of their environment to associate themselves with one or more interest groups. The number of such groups is unknown, but it surely runs into the thousands and includes organizations as diverse as the Izaak Walton League, League of Women Voters, National Conference of Christians and Jews, National Catholic Welfare Association, Veterans of Foreign Wars, Farm Bureau Federation, National Association of Manufacturers, Chamber of Commerce, National Committee for an Effective Congress, John Birch Society, AFL-CIO, and National Association of Electric Companies.

The best known and probably the most important interest groups are the economic associations representing various farm, labor, and business interests. Each of them attempts to persuade the general public, government, and political parties that there is a close, if not a one-to-one, relationship between their particular interest—improving the economic well-being of their group—and the general welfare of the citizenry. To secure both popular acceptance of their goals and governmental and political action that help achieve the goals, they conduct propaganda campaigns in newspapers and on radio and television; they lobby in Congress, the executive branch, and the judiciary; and, through campaign contributions and other forms of support, they encourage the election of politicians sympathetic to their cause.

David Truman in *The Governmental Process*, probably the best work on the subject of interest groups, provides a useful description of the nature, activities, and roles of interest groups.[4] Truman suggests that the genesis and subsequent political activity of any interest group (farm, labor, business) can be most readily understood by looking, first of all, at the origins of a single group, perhaps a simple parent-teacher association. The germ of an interest group is to be found in the tie binding the parents of all the children in a local grade school. If the school operates reasonably satisfactorily in meeting the expectations of parents and teachers, these individuals may never meet—at least they may never meet to talk about the school. However, if something happens to upset their expectations, such as the injury of a child at a crossing or instructional problems in reading and writing, the parents become understandably displeased and may call the teacher to ask for an explanation. They may also discuss the problem with other parents. If the problem is acute enough, someone might suggest, "Let's meet at my house and do something about it." At the meeting, officers may be elected and dues collected. In addition, teachers might be invited to join. Thus is born a parent-teacher association that makes demands on government for more police protection at school crossings or higher salaries for teachers. And thus is born a political interest group.

The same developmental processes observed in P.T.A. groups may be seen in the development of labor, farm, or business interest groups and their subsequent political activities. For example, after the creation of large corporations, workingmen found that they were no longer able to go directly to the boss and negotiate wage increases or improved working conditions. Instead, they were forced to complain to a foreman who often confessed his lack of authority to settle grievances without the approval of officials in New York or Cleveland or Pittsburgh. Therefore, workingmen assembled in their homes and elsewhere to grumble and to discuss ways and means of solving problems. At some meetings they elected officers, collected dues, and appointed a member to go to New York or Cleveland or Pittsburgh to bargain with the corporation officers concerning their grievances. The corporate officers sometimes refused to see the "union" representative. The "unions" then went on strike to force the company to negotiate, and eventually they asked government to force management to bargain with their representative through the National Labor Relations Act.

Political interest groups, then, emerge out of (1) events and situations which upset the expectations of individuals and groups in the society and (2) the subsequent efforts of these groups to realize their expectations or to solve the common problem which confronts them. Solution of the problem often necessitates going to the political parties and government for such things as police protection, financial aid, or restraints on the actions of other groups or individuals.

PARTY ORGANIZATION

Conceptually, the core leadership groups of political parties may be regarded as special kinds of interest groups. The leadership commonly consists of individuals and groups who use the parties as means of making claims upon other individuals and groups in the society. For purposes of classification, the reasons people join parties may be divided into two broad categories: issue-oriented motivations and non-issue-oriented motivations. The issue-oriented category includes idealists who see party activity as a means of realizing utopian goals, as well as labor and business leaders who consider party activity a tool for achieving their narrower ends of more generous wage increases or higher profits. The non-issue-oriented political activists include people in search of a government job or government contracts and those who work for a party for the "fun of it" or for ego fulfillment. As the following chapters indicate, some political party systems attract primarily job-oriented people into politics because of the plenitude of patronage available and the absence of issues in the two-party dialogue. Other systems attract primarily issue-oriented politicians because of the absence of job and patronage incentives, due, perhaps, to a state civil service system and a tradition of meaningful party competition involving contemporary problems facing the electorate.

Although most American political parties consist of individuals motivated by both issue- and non-issue-oriented ends, they have traditionally been inhabited by more job-oriented than issue-oriented people. Many political scientists as well as politicians regard the job-oriented political form as the more likely to realize the "goals of American democracy" (optimum individual freedom within a dynamic, progressive economic and social order; a government reasonably responsive to the needs of the citizenry, as expressed through their votes and their petitions, but wary of encroaching upon the "rights" of minorities). The reasoning behind the preference for job-oriented political parties is that the interest groups are the more significant units in the society and that all or almost all important issues and views are raised and represented by such groups. Therefore, the task of political parties and their leadership is to act as political brokers who bring the interest groups together; e.g., "Come, let us reason together." It is best if the political broker is impartial where issues are concerned, for he is then in a better position to act as an intermediary between labor, capital, farm, and other interests. That is, the man who is in politics simply in search of a job is in a better position to perform the special political and governmental tasks of drawing interest groups together than is the issue-oriented person who may be identified with the goals of one of the interest groups.[5]

A second reason for preferring the job-oriented political form is that it is in closer harmony with the federal form of government and the Madisonian end of dividing power and authority. The traditional job-oriented parties are oriented around the governmental patronage available at the city, county, state, and national levels. Therefore, each state party is a virtually independent entity drawing its sustenance from local patronage resources, and, consequently, the national parties in a job-oriented system are only loose confederations of fifty state political parties. Issue-oriented parties would be more unified nationally because they would be drawn together not by patronage at the local level but by a common concern with problems, thus producing a quasi-unitary rather than a federal form of government.

On the other hand, probably the majority of students of political party organizations have advocated the development of more issue-oriented parties. Their position is founded in adherence to the democratic dogma that the main function of political parties is to present clear-cut alternatives to the voters in the form of candidates and issues and, if the candidates are triumphant, to translate the majority will into law. Their objection to job-oriented parties and to the traditional organization of America's political parties is that they have not served as viable means of making democracy work.

Figure 1
Ideal Organizational Pattern of a Strong National Party

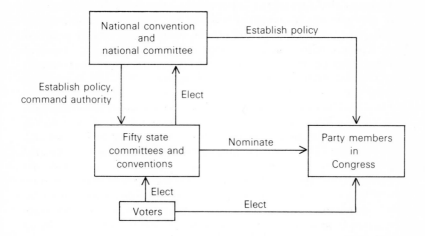

Figure 2
Actual Organizational Pattern of National Parties

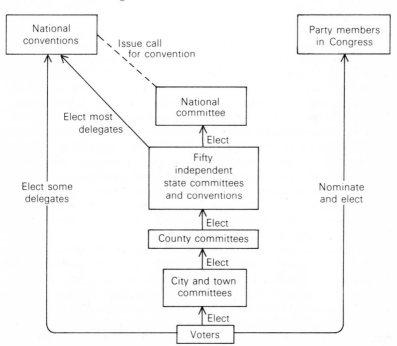

The attack of reformers on the traditional organizational structure of American politics proceeds from their commitment to democratic dogma and the belief that only by becoming centralized can the parties function effectively in terms of enabling the majority to rule. Perhaps the clearest expression of this point of view was contained in a report by the Committee on Political Parties, created by the American Political Science Association. The report stated, in part:

> Historical and other factors have caused the American two-party system to operate as two loose associations of state and local organizations, with very little national machinery and very little national cohesion. As a result, either major party, when in power, is ill-equipped to organize its members in the legislative and the executive branches into a government held together and guided by the party programs. Party responsibility at the polls thus tends to vanish. This is a very serious matter, for it affects the very heartbeat of American democracy. It also poses grave problems of domestic and foreign policy in an era when it is no longer safe for the nation to deal piecemeal with issues that can be disposed of only on the basis of coherent programs.[6]

The recommendations of the Committee stressed strengthening national party leadership through the creation of a national party council to formulate programs, publication of biennial party platforms, and elimination of the seniority rule in Congress.

The organizational ideal envisioned by the advocates of strong national parties is shown in Figure 1. In this ideal pattern, the national convention and national committee have "command" authority over all agencies of the party, including the state organizations; that is, they formulate party programs to solve the problems facing the people, and they have the authority to demand that the state parties and the elected congressmen of their party adhere to those programs. The President is visualized as the head of his party. The reformers have never solved the problem of leadership in the minority party.

The organizational reality shown in Figure 2 departs radically from the reformers' ideal. There are fifty independent state parties over which the national committee has absolutely no command authority. Further, there are 435 United States representatives and 100 United States senators, all of whom are nominated either directly by the voters or by state conventions. The national committee has absolutely no authority over the party in

Congress. However, as succeeding chapters will indicate, the informal political reality results in two national parties that are much more cohesive than Figure 2 would lead one to believe.

RELATIONSHIP OF PARTIES AND NATIONAL GOVERNMENT

The national parties might be defined as loose coalitions of state and local machines united primarily by a common desire to capture the presidency. The ability of the parties to control or influence the presidency and Congress largely determines their ability to fulfill their promises and provide a basis for the next campaign.

There are two main schools of thought concerning the relationships between the three principal American political institutions. The first view has been ably stated by Willmoore Kendall in "The Two Majorities."[7] As Kendall sees it, the President is elected by a national majority that is brought together by means of extremely nebulous platitudes and rather meaningless promises. This insubstantial foundation is a necessary condition of American politics because of the extreme diversity and broad range of needs and interests that dominate various sections of the country. On the other hand, members of Congress are elected by local majorities united by concrete and meaningful needs and aspirations. This is true because the populations of congressional districts are relatively homogeneous. Kendall concludes that a congressional majority is a more useful guide to the wishes of the people than a presidential majority.

The opposing point of view has been expressed by James M. Burns in *The Deadlock of Democracy*.[8] Burns' thesis is that America has four political parties—the presidential Democratic and Republican parties and the congressional Democratic and Republican parties—which represent different constituencies. A high proportion of all congressmen and an even higher proportion of congressional leaders come from one-party or relatively safe districts or states, while the President must appeal to more than just the members of his own party. At least until reapportionment takes full effect, this conflict is also manifested by the preponderance of presidential appeals to metropolitan areas as compared with the greater deference paid by Congress to rural and small-town areas. Burns describes the congressional parties as instruments of the Madisonian approach to government.[9] Essentially, they serve to fragment political power into 435 House districts and 100 Senate districts, each of which has rather narrow and parochial interests. The result is that Congress is incapable of thinking and working toward the solution of national problems. On the other hand, the President is elected by a majority coalition of the entire nation, which compels him to think in national rather than local terms.

Burns deplores the ability of Congress to block the President's translation of the national majority will into public policy, whereas Kendall applauds it. Basically, Burns is critical because he approves the presidential parties' policies, and Kendall concurs in congressional inaction because he disagrees with the rather liberal policies advocated by the national parties. President Johnson's success with Congress in 1965 raises questions concerning the validity of both the Kendall and Burns theses. Perhaps an explanation for Johnson's success in securing legislation from Congress may be found in reapportionment following the *Baker v. Carr* decision, the increasing nationalization of American politics, and the decline of the Republican party.

LOCAL POLITICS

In the United States, it is essential to understand state and city politics in order to develop a meaningful picture of the processes of American democracy at the national level. The division in Congress on civil rights bills, trade measures, welfare proposals, and medical care bills, for example, cannot be understood without some knowledge of Southern politics, Midwestern and border state politics, Western politics, New England politics, and big city politics.[10] The gyrations of former Senator Theodore G. Bilbo from economic liberalism to civil rights conservatism cannot be understood without an appreciation of Mississippi politics.

By way of summary, three points should be made concerning state and city politics: (1) This area of politics is important in its own right for a proper understanding of policies made at lower levels of government; (2) given the federal or decentralized character of the national parties, knowledge of this area of politics is essential for an understanding of the national political scene; and (3) the high proportion of states and districts without a fully competitive two-party system seriously affects the operation of the national parties and agencies of government, especially Congress.

In succeeding chapters, an effort is made to tie national and state politics together into a useful model of the operations of the American political system.

MINOR PARTIES

In the preceding discussion of the two-party political system in the United States, the existence of third parties was largely ignored. Third parties have often been significant features of

American election campaigns and, on occasion, have profoundly influenced the course of American political history. The Populist party of 1892, the Progressive party of 1912, the La Follette Progressive party of 1924, and the Dixiecrat party of 1948 were the four most important third-party movements in the post-Civil War period.

In all four instances, the emergence of the third party was caused by intense dissatisfaction with the policies and candidates of the two major parties. The Populists were unhappy with the hard money policies of both Democrats and Republicans, which, they felt, unduly benefited creditors in the East at the expense of debtors in the West. The Progressives of 1912 were displeased primarily with the conservative direction taken by William Howard Taft after his election in 1908; Theodore Roosevelt led the Progressives out of the Republican party in 1912 in a "Great Crusade" to reform the Republican party. The Progressives of 1924, like the Populists of 1892, looked askance at the conservatism of both the Democratic presidential candidate John W. Davis and the Republican President Calvin Coolidge; they gave voice to their unhappiness with the nomination of Robert La Follette of Wisconsin. The Dixiecrats of 1948 consisted largely of Southerners who revolted against the civil rights plank adopted in the 1948 Democratic convention, which brought to a head growing Southern dissatisfaction with the pro-civil rights biases of the Roosevelt and Truman administrations.

In each of the four third-party revolts against one or both of the major parties, the result was to push liberals toward the Democratic party and conservatives in a Republican direction. The Democrats under William Jennings Bryan adopted the Populists' program, and those under Woodrow Wilson and Franklin Roosevelt stole much of the Progressives' political thunder by including in their programs the reforms the Progressives advocated. The Republicans, on the other hand, attracted Democratic conservatives with William McKinley, who advocated retention of the gold standard in 1896, with William Howard Taft, who warded off the Progressive challenge in the 1912 Republican convention, and with Barry Goldwater, who lent a sympathetic ear to the complaints of conservative Southern Democrats in 1964.

The net effect of third-party revolts, then, has been to help divide the electorate between the two parties along the lines of contemporary issues. Whenever the political divisions of the electorate have thwarted programs designed to meet the needs of a large dissatisfied group, an ensuing third-party revolt has reshuffled the division of the electorate between the major parties.

The Socialist, Vegetarian, Prohibitionist, Socialist Labor,

Communist, and similar third parties have had little effect on the two-party system. These small bands of zealots promote narrowly conceived doctrines that have little appeal to most Americans. Consequently, the two major parties pay as little attention to them as do the voters.

APPROACHES TO THE STUDY OF POLITICAL PARTIES

Political scientists are divided roughly into three broad schools of thought concerning approaches to the study of political parties. Those in one group proudly call themselves "political behavioralists" and insist upon a rather rigid adherence to what they regard as a scientific approach to the study of politics. In practice, this means the study of quantifiable political phenomena in an effort to develop hypotheses and models concerning political behavior that are subject to validation and incorporation into broader and broader theories intended to render political phenomena more understandable and even predictable. For example, the behavioralist may begin by developing hypotheses concerning the interest group activities of the Paducah High School Parent-Teacher Association; the hypotheses may be validated and elaborated through subsequent studies of labor unions, farm organizations, and business groups; and out of them may develop certain grand theories concerning the origin, leadership, and activities of political interest groups. The behavioralist approach is relatively new, and the number of important quantifiable problems to which it can be applied remains small.

A second group of political scientists rather modestly refers to its approach to the study of politics as "barefoot empiricism." Their seeming modesty, however, is belied by their pride in a "broader," more eclectic attitude toward methodology. They use the tools of history, social psychology, sociology, biography, participant observation, or whatever else is at hand in working with political problems. They do not limit themselves to quantifiable political phenomena but quantify or "prove" wherever possible—in dealing with specific aspects of politics, such as primary elections in one-party states, for example—and resort to insight, analysis, and description where "proof" is impossible. The better studies in this category tend to be comparative and deal with the politics of cities, states, or regions (e.g., V. O. Key's *Southern Politics*). They are often narrative in form, telling the story of who rules and how they go about doing so.

The "traditional" approach to the study of political parties characterizes the third methodological grouping of political scientists. Advocates of this approach often concentrate on describing and analyzing formal political institutions, such as the organization of political parties or the steps in the enactment of legislation by Congress. They also compile biographies of political personalities or describe rather impressionistically a political campaign or event, treating both its formal aspects of organization and its informal methods of operation.[11] In the main, traditionalists reject the idea that "scientific" laws of political behavior can be developed out of an accumulation of rather narrow studies. They feel that too many variables operate on human behavior to make any important (or especially political) facet of it predictable. Instead, traditionalists attempt to understand the operations of formal political institutions by getting the "feel" of the way they actually function through an understanding of some of the personalities involved.

We turn now to brief descriptions of some of the specific techniques used by students of politics in investigating and analyzing political parties and political behavior. It should be noted that, regardless of the technique or general approach used, no one denies the desirability of using data to nail down a point wherever possible. In other words, the traditional approach to the study of politics should not be confused with sloppy research.

THE AGGREGATIVE AND ANECDOTAL APPROACH

The aggregative approach to the study of politics involves the collecting of election and other data by political units (precincts, cities, counties, states, and sections of the nation) and the use of the data in efforts to understand political processes and political behavior. For example, a study of "Negro Registration in Louisiana"[12] might begin with the collection of demographic and other data concerning the number and percentage of Negroes registered in each parish (county); the percentage of Negroes in the population; the percentage of urban, rural farm, and rural non-farm residents; the Catholic and Protestant percentages; the median family income; the proportion of tenant farmers to other farmers; a variety of election data; and any other seemingly related data. This aggregative data would enable the researcher to determine whether or not there are any important differences in the proportion of Negroes registered to vote in various parishes in Louisiana and whether or not the differences are related to Negro-white population balances, the urbanization of the parishes, their wealth, their religion, or their political preferences.

After collecting the data and discovering whether or not relationships exist among the variables, the student asks "Why?" Answers are sought through interviews with knowledgeable personalities, such as political leaders, NAACP and Citizens' Council leaders, and newspaper editors and reporters. The interviews provide the researcher with explanations (often contradictory) for the statistical relationships of his aggregative data. Where possible, he checks out the explanations by gathering new data. For example, he may be told that variations in the proportion of Negroes registered to vote are determined by local economy; i.e., in rice-growing areas the power structure tends to be pluralistic because of land ownership and land use patterns that provide Negroes with opportunities for political activity, whereas in cotton-producing areas where land is owned by a few of the gentry the power structure is monolithic, thus minimizing Negro political opportunities unless the large landholders happen to support Negro aspirations. It is simple to test such hypotheses by obtaining data on the type of farming done in each parish and, using simple correlation techniques, noting whether or not rice farming is positively related to Negro registration. Of course, a significant positive relationship between per cent of population engaged in rice farming and per cent of Negro registration would not prove a causative relationship between the two variables. Any number of phenomena might be involved, and the conscientious researcher includes other possible causative factors in his analysis and uses multiple and partial correlation techniques to test their independent relationships to Negro registration.

The aggregative and anecdotal approach is generally used by the methodological middle-of-the-roaders—i.e., the barefoot empiricists. Frequently, their statistical tools are rather crude by the standards of statisticians because of the sometimes limited professional ability of the researchers and because interviews are used as the bases for hypotheses which may be quantitatively confirmed but which are often used as unconfirmed but plausible explanations of statistical or observed relationships between variables.

The advantage of this approach is that it lends itself to the comparative study of large political entities, which, when well done, can present interesting correlations and analyses as well as an unstatistical facet of real life. The disadvantage is the large residue of unsupported assumptions in the studies and the sometimes frequent failure of researchers to clearly label these assumptions as such.

THE SAMPLE SURVEY APPROACH

The sample survey approach to political behavior involves the collection of data by means of questions directed at a "scientifically" selected portion of the population under study. It differs from aggregative data in that the sampler can better and more directly determine how members of certain groups voted. After the survey is completed, he knows, for example, that 486 of the 521 Negroes in the sample said they voted for Johnson in 1964. The researcher with aggregative data, on the other hand, can say only that in precincts which are 90 per cent or more Negro, Johnson received, say, 88 per cent of the vote; he has no way of knowing which Negroes in his precincts voted for Johnson and, in fact, cannot be certain of the precise proportion of the vote cast by Negroes.

The sample survey is generally limited to gathering citizen opinions and determining the relationships of those opinions to demographic and other data obtained through interviews, although it may also include information on questions for which the aggregator must seek indirect and hypothetical answers. In contrast to the aggregative and anecdotal approach, the sample survey alone seldom contributes much toward a fuller understanding of political processes—who rules and how do they go about it? who gets what and from whom is it taken?—but must be supplemented by studies of formal and informal political organization.

The administration of a sample survey involves several rather basic steps, which are a great deal more difficult to execute in practice than to state in theory. The first step is to determine what is to be studied and why. The subject might be student opinion at the University of Massachusetts concerning American policy toward Vietnam. The reasons for the research include curiosity (an important motivation for all researchers) and a desire to test certain hypotheses concerning opinions in general and student opinions in particular—e.g., to prove that opinion is related to group affiliation and level of information by comparing the responses of seniors and freshmen, of humanities majors and professional school majors, of students who identified themselves as Democrats with those who called themselves Republicans, of those who were well informed about events in Vietnam as measured by a series of objective questions (What is the capital of South Vietnam? North Vietnam? etc.) with those who were poorly informed. The researcher must state his hypotheses and objectives in concrete terms and develop a questionnaire eliciting responses which, when analyzed, will either support or refute the hypotheses.

The second step in the administration of a sample survey is to determine the *universe* from which the sample is to be taken; in the example, the statement of the research objective defined the universe as the student body of the University of Massachusetts.

Next, the size of the sample to be drawn from the universe is decided in light of the level of accuracy required and the resources available for the study. The final decision in the study cited was to draw a sample of one hundred opinions because only twenty students volunteered to administer the questionnaire and because the need for pinpoint accuracy was not great.

The third step is to draw the sample in a *random* fashion so that every person in the universe has an equal chance of being included among the respondents to the questionnaire. It was possible to draw a sample of students at the University of Massachusetts in very nearly random fashion (the only departure being the alphabetical listing) by using the student directory and dividing the entire number of students (9500) by 100. The first student was selected from the directory by putting the numbers 1-95 in a hat and drawing one; if the number was 43, then the 43rd student listed became the first respondent, the 138th student (43 + 95) the second respondent, and so on.

The next three steps are to pretest the questionnaire, administer the questionnaire, and analyze the data. It was necessary to pretest the questionnaire on fellow students to be certain that the questions were clear and elicited the desired information. It was also useful to consult with a person in the data processing center to be certain that the responses could be easily coded and punched on cards for the computer. This simplified totaling the responses and working out relationships between opinions on Vietnam and group memberships.

The final step is for the researcher to communicate his data to his audience in a readable and intelligible form. This usually involves making clear statements of the objectives of the study, the preliminary hypotheses or assumptions, and the results which support, refute, or raise questions about the hypotheses.

The sample survey is a valuable research tool of the social scientist, and when combined with panel studies and controlled experiments, it enables students to find answers to very difficult social science problems. For example, a student of propaganda can select two samples of a universe, matching the two groups as perfectly as possible with respect to age, sex, income, religion, ethnic background, and any other variables he may feel are significant. He can then test both groups for their opinons concerning anti-Semitism, and he should find that very nearly identical proportions of the two samples are tolerant and anti-Semitic. He might next expose one of the samples (the experimental group) to a propaganda film in favor of tolerance, while the other sample (the control group) would not see the film. Afterward, he would test both groups a second time. Presumably, any differences found in the opinions between the first and second tests would be the result of the film.

Typically, students of politics who use sample surveys classify themselves as behavioralists, meaning that they use the "scientific" approach to the study of political behavior. However, all students of politics, including barefoot empiricists and traditionalists, use the results of their research. *The American Voter*,[13] which reports much of the data compiled by the University of Michigan Survey Research Center, is representative of the virtues and limitations of the sample survey approach. It helps nail down many hypotheses concerning political behavior, taking them out of the realm of hunches and airy theories. On the other hand, it contributes little to the student's understanding of the struggle for power that is at the heart of politics, because of the authors' reluctance to interpret their "facts."

THE MODEL BUILDING APPROACH

Every professor builds a model of sorts of his subject matter. A model is a simplified construct of the subject being studied. By nature, models focus on the certain processes and forces believed to be determinative of what happens. Their purpose is to isolate what is basic, fundamental, and therefore significantly causative and thereby to eliminate the trivial and the accidental, which may confuse or divert the observer in the real world. A model that closely duplicates reality can be very helpful to the student in understanding a complex economic system or the un-seen world of atomic particles, but a carelessly constructed model can be badly misleading. Another danger is that models are often mistaken for reality.

In a sense, professors are iconoclasts, reflecting the need of each generation to smash or revise the models of the past genera-tion in the light of new knowledge or a changed reality. Be that as it may, the model, so long employed in economics, has now been introduced to the field of political parties. Anthony Downs' *An Economic Theory of Democracy*[14] represents an effort to adapt an economist's model of the economic system to the operations of a political system. Downs begins with the assumption that man is a rational economic animal who prefers the greater good to the lesser good. He further assumes that political parties are led by people whose primary purpose is to win political office—i.e., that they are job-oriented rather than issue-oriented. Therefore, they act essentially as entrepreneurs in attempting to sell their party and candidates to the voters. Further, voters are consumers who attempt to maximize their returns from their votes.

Downs then constructs a model of the party system (based upon these and other assumptions) that provides interesting insights into political behavior. He answers the inevitable question concerning the distance of the model from reality by pointing to the similarity between the behavior of the actors in the model and political behavior in the real world.

THE PARTICIPANT–OBSERVATION APPROACH

The participant-observation approach to the study of political parties is, in effect, a traditional means of understanding political processes and systems. The literature is replete with descriptions of political events by students of politics who observed and/or participated in a campaign or in the organization of a party.[15] The studies usually place first emphasis on descriptions of behavior, processes, and systems. The descriptions may provide raw material for the later formulation of hypotheses concerning, for example, the locus of power or the behavior of politicians and voters.

Theodore Abel, in an interesting article entitled "An Operation Called Verstehen,"[16] identifies one limitation of the participant-observation approach. According to Abel, scholars who use this approach tend to apply old experiences and knowledge in explaining new situations. Abel's example is the person who observes a neighbor lighting a fire in his fireplace as the first snowflakes of winter drift to the ground in November. The observer applies his own experience and knowledge to his neighbor's behavior and assumes that he is lighting the fire because it is cold. In fact, of course, the neighbor may be lighting the fire out of a desire to call attention to his new fireplace, or because he is a pyromaniac, or to provide a suitable setting for *amour,* or any of another hundred reasons or some complex combination of them all. Thus, the original assumption is naught but a plausible hypothesis that must be tested — through a psychiatric examination of the neighbor. Actually, Abel's criticism is not an indictment of the participation-observation approach but only of the techniques employed by some of its practitioners. The descriptions derived from such studies are undeniably valuable in understanding political systems and processes, and the insights provided are useful in the formulation of broad hypotheses concerning political behavior and political systems.

The only real problem with the approach has been the tendency of some students to assume the validity of their hypotheses without testing them. Floyd Hunter's *Community Power Structure,*[17] a study of leadership in Atlanta, Georgia, described an interesting attempt to validate a hypothesis by interviewing participants in the life of a community. Hunter attempted to determine whether or not a pyramidal power structure (in which only a few people rule) existed in Atlanta by using such devices as counting the number of times knowledgeable people in that city named a person as a power figure. A more recent attempt to validate hypotheses concerning power structures was Robert Dahl's study of New Haven, Connecticut, entitled *Who Governs?*[18] Hunter concluded that a pyramidal power structure did exist in Atlanta; Dahl concluded that New Haven had a pluralistic (a great many or diffused points of power) power structure.

An early attempt to go beyond participant-observation and to validate the hypotheses emerging therefrom is contained in William F. Whyte's *Street Corner Society*.[19] Whyte lived in a low-income Italian neighborhood for some years in an effort to analyze leadership in small groups. He became a member of a gang in the neighborhood and thus was able intimately to observe patterns of leadership. He attempted to quantify his observations by such devices as counting the number of times various members of the group interacted and analyzing the circumstances of their inter-action. Further, he quantified some of his observations concerning the effect of the group and its leadership patterns on the behavior of its members. For example, he found that some of the low-status members were excellent bowlers when playing by themselves or with people outside the group but that when they bowled with the group their scores generally corresponded to their "pecking order" in the Street Corner Society. The reason, according to Whyte, was that they were heckled when they threatened to out-score a high-status member of the group. Abel would add that Whyte should test this hypothesis.

CONCLUSIONS

In summary, the students of political parties tend to con-centrate on certain aspects of party organizations. Some study the formal structures of the parties, of interest groups, or of the parties in the legislature. Other students attempt to develop a broader understanding of the ways in which political parties actually function through biographies of prominent politicians, case histories, or participant-observation studies. Still others try to penetrate more deeply into the subject by validating or in-validating hypotheses and by developing theories of political behavior that provide the students of politics with models that are ever closer to reality.

The ultimate purpose of all political research is to enable the student to understand and thus to cope more effectively with the political aspect of his environment, whether it be the political side of his job or the politics of town, state, or national government. The purpose of the following chapters of this study of American two-party politics is to provide a model of the political world that will make it more understandable.

Two-Party Competition: Does It Make a Difference?

There are one hundred state political parties and thousands of semi-independent county and city parties in the United States. These state parties and their subdivisions join one of two giant political confederations, called the Democratic and Republican national parties, in quadrennial efforts to elect a President and a Vice-President of the United States. The state parties have a permanence and a clarity of power structure lacking in the national parties, and their character shapes the national parties. Therefore, an understanding of American political parties demands some acquaintance with the state parties.

There are many possible ways in which to classify state parties, such as by sections, but the most meaningful classification would seem to be by categories of party competition. Our concern with state parties is primarily to discover the forms they take, their impact on governmental policy, and their effects on the national political parties. Using these ends as guides, we will first examine the issue-oriented two-party states, then the traditional job-oriented two-party states, and then the one-party states. Finally we will attempt to develop a meaningful portrayal of the two major national political parties as related to and affected by the state parties.

Not a great deal has been done in the way of sharply differentiating among the three types of state political systems. As stated in Chapter One, the main distinction between the two kinds of two-party systems is that people in programmatic, or issue-oriented, parties enter politics because they see political jobs as the means of securing policy goals they regard as desirable, whereas people join traditional job-oriented parties largely out of a desire for office and perceive the issues as means of getting into office. In one-party states the struggle over who shall rule obviously takes place within a single dominant party. V. O. Key in *Southern Politics*[1] found that in some one-party states this struggle is usually between two fairly well defined factions. In such states, the bifactional battles closely resemble those of two-party systems, except that primaries replace elections. In other Southern states that have no well-defined factions, the result is an amorphous political system that comes closer to no-party or multiparty politics than to one-party politics.

Students of politics generally assume that two-party politics is preferable to one-party politics and that issue-oriented two-party politics is superior to job-oriented two-party politics. It would seem desirable, then, to examine the following assumptions: (1) that two-party state politics measurably affects the performance of state government and (2) that issue-oriented two-party politics is more likely to make a difference in the objective performance of government than is the traditional two-party variety.[2]

The literature abounds in assumptions concerning the virtues of two-party competition that are difficult if not impossible to measure, such as that it results in more honest government. However, a central consequence believed to result from two-party competition does lend itself to quantitative analysis. According to most observers, two-party competition almost invariably leads to appeals for the support of lower-income voters because they are so numerous, while other political systems tend to be more oligarchical and less responsive to the needs and desires of the poor. Consequently, it is believed, two-party competition is more likely to lead to subsequent governmental actions addressed to these needs. If this assumption is true, it should be reflected in relative levels of governmental expenditure, particularly for items such as welfare and public education, which are designed to reduce inequalities in the distribution of goods and opportunities.

DIFFERENTIAL INTENSITY OF COMPETITION

Starting, then, with the notion that a great deal of two-party competition will be accompanied by relatively greater state expenditures on welfare and education, the first requirement was to test this hypothesis. The problem was to somehow differentiate among the states in terms of the intensity of two-party competition and then to see how much the states spent on welfare and education. A few earlier exploratory efforts in this direction had been made,[3] but none had been successfully addressed to the problem of separating two-party competition from other variables, such as urban and income, that also influence levels of state expenditures on welfare programs, and the studies had largely ignored the difference between two-party job-oriented and two-party issue-oriented competition. Further, the measures of competition had concentrated on two-party divisions in gubernatorial elections and thus had overlooked the important role of the legislatures, particularly their vetoes of programs proposed by the governors. Most important, perhaps, the earlier studies had overlooked legislative malapportionment, which could produce one-party politics in the legislatures even where the states were fairly evenly divided between the parties.

In order to overcome these earlier shortcomings, two-party competition was measured by averaging, for each state, the percentage of Republican and Democratic votes cast in each gubernatorial election and the percentage of Republican and Democratic seats in each of the two state legislative houses for the period from 1946 through 1958 (Nebraska and Minnesota were excluded from the study because their legislative elections are nonpartisan). The result for a state might be a 52-48 average percentage division in the gubernatorial elections and a 60-40 average division of the two houses of the legislature. The competition score adopted was the sum of the two lesser percentages— 88 in the example. A one-party state, then, in which the average division both in the gubernatorial elections and in the legislature was 100-0, would have a competition score of zero. On the other hand, a very evenly competitive two-party state, in which both average percentage divisions were 50-50, would have a score of 100. Most states, of course, ranged between these two extremes of no competition and perfect competition.

Table I presents the competition scores, which will surprise few readers. The least competitive states, those at the bottom of the scale, are one-party Southern states. Slightly higher are the weak two-party states in New England, the Midwest, and the border states. At the top of the competition scale are most of the

TABLE I

Rank of States According to Two-Party Competition Score

States[a]	Competition Score[b]	States	Competition Score
Montana	97	New Hampshire	71
Washington	97	Kentucky	69
Massachusetts	96	Kansas	68
Nevada	95	Maine	65
Delaware	95	Iowa	64
Utah	92	Arizona	64
Rhode Island	91	South Dakota	60
Colorado	91	Oklahoma	54
Idaho	90	Vermont	50
Pennsylvania	90	North Dakota	45
California	89	Virginia	42
Illinois	89	North Carolina	37
New Jersey	88	Tennessee	34
Connecticut	87	Florida	24
Missouri	87	Arkansas	19
Wyoming	85	Alabama	15
New York	84	Texas	10
Indiana	83	Louisiana	01
Michigan	80	Georgia	01
West Virginia	78	Mississippi	00
Ohio	77	South Carolina	00
New Mexico	76		
Maryland	75		
Wisconsin	73		
Oregon	72		

[a]Nebraska and Minnesota were excluded from the study because their legislative elections are non-partisan.

[b]Competition scores were derived by averaging, for the period 1946–1958, the percentage of Republican and Democratic votes cast in gubernatorial elections and the percentage of Republican and Democratic seats in the state legislatures. The final score for each state is the sum of the two lesser percentages. For gubernatorial election data by states, 1946–1958, see Richard Scammon, *America Votes* (Pittsburgh: University of Pittsburgh Press, 1959), Vol. III. For statistics on party divisions in the state legislatures, see *Book of the States* (Chicago: Council of State Governments), published biannually.

Western states and the industrial states of the Northeast and Midwest. Some readers may be disturbed by the relatively low ranking of those states commonly thought of as extremely competitive two-party states, such as Ohio (21), Michigan (19), and New York (17). The cause is malapportionment of the state legislatures, which produced one-sided Republican majorities even when Democrats controlled the governorship. The rankings will also suggest to the sophisticated reader that many dimensions of two-party competition, especially the degree to which it is issue-oriented, have not been sharply measured. (See pages 46-49 of this chapter for some measures of the issue-oriented content of state politics.)

EFFECTS OF COMPETITION AND OTHER VARIABLES ON GOVERNMENT PERFORMANCE

COMPETITION

The next step in the effort to discover whether two-party competition has some measurable impact on the performance of state government was to measure specific categories of state and local expenditures for welfare and education. The categories selected were per capita welfare expenditures, excluding federal grants-in-aid, 1959; per recipient Aid to Dependent Children payments, November 1960; per pupil expenditures for education, 1959-1960; and total per capita general expenditures (all state and local for all purposes) excluding federal grants-in-aid, 1959. The expenditures of state and local governments were combined because of the enormous differences among states in their allocations of these responsibilities between the two levels of government.

After obtaining these measures of state and local government expenditures, it was necessary to relate them to the competition scores. The states were divided into three degrees of competitiveness: strong two-party (80-100 competition score), weak two-party (40-79), and one-party (0-39). The average expenditures in each of the four welfare categories were then compared with each of these three competition levels. The results, shown in Table II, strongly support the assumption that two-party competition affects the performance of state government. In each of the selected categories, the group of strong two-party states spent more than did the group of weak two-party states, and the weak two-party states as a group were more generous than were the one-party states.

TABLE II

Relation Between Two-Party Competition and Per Capita State and Local Welfare Expenditures

Intervals of competition scores	Number of states	Average per capita welfare expenditure, 1959[a]	Average per recipient aid to dependent children payments, November 1960[b]	Average education expenditure per pupil in ADA, 1959–1960[c]	Average total per capita general expenditure, 1959[a]
80–100 (strong two-party)	19	$13.10	$37.87	$241.21	$262.48
40–79 (weak two-party)	17	9.32	32.98	205.14	224.02
0–39 (one-party)	10	6.68	17.00	143.15	181.85

[a]U.S. Department of Commerce. Bureau of the Census. *Governmental Finances in 1959.*
[b]U.S. Department of Health, Education, and Welfare. Bureau of Public Assistance. Division of Program Statistics and Analysis. *Advance Release of Public Assistance, November 1960.*
[c]Research Division, National Education Association. *Rankings of the States, 1960.*
ADA means "average daily attendance."

WEALTH

However, further examination of the competitive ranking of the states raised several doubts concerning the meaning of Table II. A second look at Table I reveals that the more competitive states tend also to be the wealthier and more urban states, whereas the states at the bottom of the scale tend to be the poorest and least urban. One question, then, was whether Table II showed merely that the wealthier states spend more money and that they do so because they can more readily afford to, rather than because of party competition.

This problem of the relation between party competition and per capita wealth was met by dividing the strongly competitive, weakly competitive, and one-party states into high per capita income, middle per capita income, and low per capita income groups. This division made it possible to compare the expenditures of wealthy strong two-party states with those of wealthy weak two-party states (there were no high-income one-party states), and the expenditures of middle-income and low-income strong two-party states with those of middle-income and low-income weak two-party states and with those of middle-income and low-income one-party states.

When this method was followed with respect to welfare, Aid to Dependent Children, and per pupil expenditures, the results once again generally confirmed the hypothesis that two-party competition does influence the level and kinds of governmental programs. Reference to Tables III, IV, and V reveals that in every instance the group of wealthy strong two-party states spent more for these programs than did wealthy weak two-party states, that the group of middle-income strong two-party states tended to spend more than did middle-income weak two-party states, and that the group of middle-income weak two-party states spent more than middle-income one-party states. The same relationships prevailed among the groups of low-income states: strongly competitive states tended to spend more than weak two-party states, and weak two-party states spent more than one-party states.

URBANISM

At this point, then, the wealth variable had been separated from party competition, and the statistical exercise had demonstrated an independent competition effect on certain types of governmental expenditures. However, as revealed by Table VI, competition is related to urbanism as well as to per capita income, which raises the question of the degree to which urbanism may be

TABLE III

Relation Between Two-Party Competition, Income, and Per Capita State and Local Welfare Expenditures, 1959

Intervals of competition scores	High income		Middle income		Low income	
	Number of states	Average per capita welfare expenditure*	Number of states	Average per capita welfare expenditure*	Number of states	Average per capita welfare expenditure*
80–100 (strong two-party)	12	$14.24	6	$11.66	1	$8.13
40–79 (weak two-party)	3	10.01	7	9.01	7	9.32
0–39 (one-party)	0	——	2	6.71	8	6.67

*U.S. Department of Commerce, Bureau of the Census. *Governmental Finances in 1959.*

TABLE IV

Relation Between Two-Party Competition, Income, and Per Recipient Aid to Dependent Children Payments, 1960

Intervals of competition scores	High income		Middle income		Low income	
	Number of states	Average per recipient ADC payments*	Number of states	Average per recipient ADC payments*	Number of states	Average per recipient ADC payments*
80–100 (strong two-party)	12	$40.01	6	$33.02	1	$41.22
40–79 (weak two-party)	3	33.56	7	35.75	7	29.97
0–39 (one-party)	0	——	2	17.24	8	16.92

*U.S. Department of Health, Education, and Welfare, Bureau of Public Assistance, Division of Program Statistics and Analysis, *Advance Release of Public Assistance, November 1960.*

TABLE V

Relation of Two-Party Competition and Income to Education Expenditures Per Pupil in ADA, 1959–1960

Intervals of competition scores	High income		Middle income		Low income	
	Number of states	Average expenditure per pupil*	Number of states	Average expenditure per pupil*	Number of states	Average expenditure per pupil*
80–100 (strong two-party)	12	$251.23	6	$222.93	1	$230.53
40–79 (weak two-party)	3	232.09	7	215.20	7	183.52
0–39 (one-party)	0	—	2	195.07	8	130.16

*Research Division, National Education Association, *Rankings of the States, 1960.*

TABLE VI

Relation of Two-Party Competition to Average Per Capita Income and to Average Percentage of Urban Residents

Intervals of competition scores	Number of states	Average per capita income, 1959[a]	Average per cent urban residents, 1960[b]
80–100 (strong two-party)	19	$2404	72.6
40–79 (weak two-party)	17	1960	55.9
0–39 (one-party)	10	1555	53.6

[a]U.S. Bureau of the Census, *Statistical Abstract of the United States, 1961.*
[b]U.S. Bureau of the Census, *County and City Data Book, 1962.*

the causative factor underlying the relationships found between party competition and governmental expenditures for welfare and education. The next problem was therefore to find a means of isolating the effects of two-party competition from both income and urbanism. The method selected was to compute simple and multiple correlations for each of the expenditure variables.

The reader should not throw up his hands in despair at the mention of simple and multiple correlations. Basically, all they do is show in numerical terms the degree to which two or more variables are associated. For example, in the 1960 presidential election, if State A was 1.1 per cent Catholic and gave Kennedy 1.1 per cent of its total vote, and if State B was 95.6 per cent Catholic and gave Kennedy 95.6 per cent of its vote, and if State C was 44.2 per cent Catholic and gave Kennedy 44.2 per cent of its total vote, and if this same relationship between the Catholic percentage of the population and Kennedy's percentage of the vote prevailed in every other state, then there would be a perfect simple correlation between the two variables. Such a one-to-one relationship between two variables is expressed, in terms of a simple coefficient of correlation, as an *r* of 1.0. An *r* of 0.9 or 0.8 would reflect a close but not perfect correlation. If there were little relationship at all, the *r* would be 0.1 or (-)0.1 or 0.2 or 0.3.

Similarly, the multiple correlation is a mathematical computation designed to analyze and summarize the relationship between one variable and two or more other variables. For example, in the 1960 election Kennedy received most of the Catholic vote, the vote of the foreign born, and most of the urban votes (there is considerable overlap among the three variables). If the fluctuation in the vote Kennedy received in each state were perfectly related to fluctuations in the three variables of per cent Catholic, per cent foreign born, and per cent urban, then a multiple correlation would reveal an R of 1.0. If the relationship were close but not perfect, then the R might be 0.9 or 0.8, as in the case of simple correlations.

The multiple correlation has an additional utility that is particularly important here. It is possible after computing a multiple correlation to find the percentage that each variable contributed to the total relationship. In the example cited, it might be found that Catholicism contributed to 30 per cent of the relationship with Kennedy's vote, foreign birth to 40 per cent, and urbanism to 30 per cent.

The problem in the present study was to find the relationship between state and local welfare expenditures and the three significant variables—two-party competition, urbanism, and per capita income—and to determine whether two-party competition represented an important part of the total relationship. Similarly, it was necessary to perform the same operation with Aid to Dependent Children, education, and total general expenditures. A preliminary part of the process was to compute the simple correlations between each of the seven variables. This operation was useful, for it confirmed the evidence in the statistically cruder Tables II-V. As shown by Table VII, there proved to be a significant positive relationship among all seven of the variables: the relationship was significant in that it was large enough numerically to virtually exclude the possibility that it was due to chance (1 per cent level of significance = .372); and the relationship was positive in that where one of the variables tended to be high, the others also tended to be high, and where one was low, the others also tended to be low. The coefficients of correlation indicate that the more competitive states tend also to be the wealthier and more urban states and that the states which spend the most on welfare, education, Aid to Dependent Children, and total general expenditures also tend to be the more competitive, wealthier, and more urban states.

Table VII, then, statistically verifies the inferences tentatively drawn from the preceding tables, but the problem of isolating the effects of the variables remained. The figures obtained from multiple correlations, shown in Table VIII, isolate them by relating the three variables of two-party competition, per capita income, and per cent urbanism to each of the four measures of

TABLE VII

Simple Coefficients of Correlation of Seven Variables for 46 States (1% level of significance = .372)

	Competition (1)	Income (2)	Urbanism (3)	Welfare (4)	ADC (5)	Per pupil (6)	Total general (7)
(1) Competition	—	.738	.478	.479	.723	.693	.552
(2) Income	.738	—	.784	.543	.621	.776	.761
(3) Urbanism	.478	.784	—	.529	.483	.589	.536
(4) Welfare	.479	.543	.529	—	.588	.541	.669
(5) ADC	.723	.621	.483	.588	—	.778	.653
(6) Per pupil	.693	.776	.589	.541	.778	—	.818
(7) Total general	.552	.761	.536	.669	.653	.818	—

TABLE VIII

Multiple Correlation of Selected Expenditure Variables with Competition, Income, and Urbanism for 46 States
(1% level of significance = .244)

Expenditures	R^2	Relative importance (by per cent) in the R^2 relationship*		
		Competition	Income	Urbanism
Welfare	.348	36.1	15.0	48.9
ADC	.548	75.4	6.1	18.5
Education	.634	31.6	66.1	2.3
Total general	.590	(−)5.1	80.2	(−)14.7

*Percentages refer to the relative importance of each independent variable in the total correlation relationships. That is, competition represents 36.1% of the .348 R^2 relationship of competition, income, and urbanism with welfare; income represents 15.0% of that relationship; and so on. The apportionment of relative importance is taken from H. A. Wallace and G. W. Snedecor, *Correlation and Machine Calculation,* Iowa State College Official Publication, Vol. XXX, No. 4 (June 24, 1931), pp. 28–29.

governmental expenditures and by including the percentage that each of the three variables contributes to the relationship. The column headed by the notation R^2 provides an arithmetic expression of the relationship of the three significant variables to each expenditure variable; R^2 is used in the table instead of R because it more accurately indicates the closeness of the relationship between the three significant variables and the expenditure variable. For example, the R for the relationship of welfare expenditures to competition, income, and urbanism is .634, which exaggerates the closeness of the relationship. The R^2 for welfare expenditures, on the other hand, tells that almost 35 per cent of the fluctuations in welfare expenditures from state to state was related to fluctuations in competition, per capita income, and per cent urbanism.

The data thus showed that two-party competition does have a measurable effect on the levels of welfare, Aid to Dependent Children, and per pupil expenditures independent of both urbanism and income. The independent impact of degree of two-party competition on level of expenditures varied from Aid to Dependent Children, where 75 per cent of the total association was attributable to competition, to education expenditures, where 32 per cent of the total association was attributable to competition. Nevertheless, the results were sufficiently significant to warrant our entering upon a study of American politics with the fairly confident assumption that two-party competition does indeed importantly affect the relative size of selected governmental programs.

Interestingly, the multiple correlation indicated quite convincingly that competition does not have much effect on the total amount spent by state and local governments but that 80 per cent of the relationship between the three significant variables and total general expenditures is attributable to variations in per capita income. In other words, the wealthier the state, the more it spent *in toto*. Thus, competition would appear to influence the *direction* (e.g., highways vs. welfare or education) rather than the amount of expenditures, with strongly competitive states tending to allocate a larger share of their fiscal pies to the categories that reallocate goods and opportunities. The evidence thus seems to support the notion that party competition focuses on, and causes greater concern about, certain kinds of welfare and education programs than is the case in other kinds of politics. It is not proven, but it is a logical and persuasive conclusion, that this tendency is a result of the fact that party competition "democratizes" politics by paying greater deference to the poor and thereby rendering politics less oligarchical.

PARTY ORIENTATION

Undoubtedly, there are many variables in addition to competition, urbanism, and income that influence the amount and direction of state expenditures, such as the national origins of the population; the relationships of governments with state universities; accidents of personality in the governors' offices; the levels of expectation about expenditures; the aspirations for political advancement of governors, particularly in the more populous and politically pivotal states; differences in urban-rural proportions; and relations between state and national parties. However, the principal remaining concern of this study was the possible independent influence of issue-oriented politics as opposed to traditional job-oriented politics on the level and direction of expenditures.

The preceding data have established quite persuasively that two-party competitive politics tends to be more issue-oriented than other kinds of political systems, at least within the borders of the United States, and that two-party competition does not affect levels of total governmental expenditures but only their direction. However, impressionistic observation of the American political scene uncovers examples of states with one-party systems, such as Louisiana, whose governments spend large sums on public programs and especially on welfare and education. Therefore, it would seem that, to a degree at least, issue-oriented politics may be independent of the two-party political form.

Table IX isolates those states in which issue-oriented politics exists independent of the two-party form. The states are ranked according to the proportion of per capita income collected as per capita state and local tax revenues. In a sense, the table measures the degree to which the citizens of the state agree with John Galbraith that the marginal return from public expenditures will be greater than the return from private expenditures. The hope in constructing the table was that, by identifying the states that spend the most and the least on public expenditures relative to income, it would be possible to isolate the factor or factors responsible for issue-oriented politics.

The measure of governmental vs. private allocation of income employed in Table IX was not significantly related to competition [(-).137], income [(-).314], or urbanism [(-).319].* The results

---

*A minus figure preceding a coefficient of correlation signifies that as you get more of one variable, you find less of the other. For example, in 1960 there was a negative relationship between the per cent Protestant in a community and the per cent vote received by Kennedy.

TABLE IX

Per Capita Government Expenditures Relative to Per Capita Income, 1959

States	Rank*	States	Rank
South Dakota	1	Michigan	26
North Dakota	2	Georgia	27
Vermont	3	New Hampshire	28
Louisiana	4	Rhode Island	29
Wyoming	5	Tennessee	30
Montana	6	North Carolina	31
Kansas	7	South Carolina	32
Mississippi	8	Indiana	33
Colorado	9	Alabama	34
California	10	Maryland	35
Idaho	11	Texas	36
Maine	12	New Jersey	37
Iowa	13	West Virginia	38
Massachusetts	14	Kentucky	39
Arizona	15	Connecticut	40
New Mexico	16	Pennsylvania	41
Oklahoma	17	Ohio	42
Washington	18	Virginia	43
Oregon	19	Illinois	44
Utah	20	Missouri	45
Wisconsin	21	Delaware	46
New York	22		
Arkansas	23		
Nevada	24		
Florida	25		

*The rank order of states is based on the percentage of per capita income collected as per capita state and local tax revenue from own sources (i.e., revenue gathered from within the state, exclusive of federal grant-in-aid and other funds).

were somewhat surprising, because if expenditures for governmental programs were largely a function of the expectations of people concerning the content of good welfare, education, highway, and other programs, then one would expect a more pronounced negative correlation of the proportion of income allocated to government to (1) the wealth of the state and (2) per cent urbanism. The assumption would be that in states such as

California and New York (high-income urban states), the government could easily meet public expectations with respect to education, welfare, and highway programs, whereas in states such as Arkansas and Kentucky (low-income rural states), the government would be forced to make heroic efforts to meet those expectations. Since the proportion of per capita income allocated to government through tax revenue was also negatively related to competition, the correlation tends to confirm the notion that the level of government vs. private expenditure is at least partially determined by factors somewhat independent of the three variables measured. The most dramatic evidence of the validity of this hypothesis is provided by the politics of the twelve states that ranked lowest in effort (i.e., government expenditure). Four of the bottom twelve states were competitive two-party states— Pennsylvania, Ohio, Illinois, and Delaware. Five were one-party or very weak two-party states—Texas, West Virginia, Kentucky, Virginia, and Missouri. Midwestern, Southern, and Eastern states are also represented among the last twelve states. In addition, the bottom twelve states differ greatly in their levels of per capita income and urbanization, their religious compositions, their proportions of foreign-born citizens, and their economies.

However, eleven of the last twelve states have one important characteristic in common. In each one, with the single exception of Connecticut,[4] the composition of both the Democratic and Republican parties is in part a function of the Civil War. People from the South who settled in those states often sympathized with the South during the Civil War and voted Democratic, and settlers from New England voted Republican in support of Abraham Lincoln. The political loyalties that developed out of the Civil War persist in the 1960's through the sons and grandsons of the original settlers, which means that current political affiliations have little relevance to current issues. Thus, in these states, class and other divisions of the electorate concerning twentieth-century issues are obscured and distorted by the white supremacy issue and by the sectional division produced by the Civil War, and the consequence in all eleven states has been an almost unbroken history of standpattism and oligarchical rule.

Among the high-effort states, it is interesting to note that many are one-party or weak two-party states—e.g., North Dakota, South Dakota, Vermont, Louisiana, and Mississippi. Again, the one-party character of these states is largely a product of the Civil War, when the population was almost unanimously committed to either the Union or the Confederacy. Therefore, subsequent political divisions within these one-party states have tended to be within the single dominant party, and these divisions have been caused by twentieth-century events. In some cases a division has been along class and other economic lines—e.g., the Longs vs. Standard Oil and the business community in Louisiana, and the farmer-laborites vs. the railroads and other business interests in North and South Dakota. It should also be noted that many of the high-effort states are located in the Western United States, where the Civil War had little impact on political divisions and where party affiliation similarly tends to be based on twentieth-century issues.

CONCLUSIONS

Thus, both the hypotheses that served as initial guidelines for this study of American politics have some statistical support. First, we have shown that there is a significant statistical relation between two-party competition and expenditures for education and welfare. Then, through statistical tabulations and historical and quantitative analyses of individual states, we have found that in states whose political divisions are related to current issues, expenditures relative to wealth are likely to be greater than in states whose political divisions are based on historical issues. Consequently, both two-party competition and issue-oriented politics were found to be related to the measurable fiscal behavior of state and local governments.

In subsequent chapters we will examine in some detail the characteristics of the various kinds of state political party systems and their effects on public opinion, state governments, and the relationships of governments with interest groups. We will then bring together the one hundred state party pieces in an attempt to provide an understandable and realistic portrayal of the national two-party mosaic.

The analyses should provide guidance to students of politics concerning the virtues and vices of the several party systems—two-party issue-oriented, two-party job-oriented, one-party. In the field of political science as well as in the popular press, there has been much adulation of two-party competition with little firm knowledge of its forms or its effects. It is hoped that the succeeding pages will help students of government to decide whether the returns from various kinds of political competition offset the considerable cost and effort expended to maintain two viable and competitive political parties.

Two-Party
Issue-Oriented Politics

An issue-oriented two-party system consists of competing groups of people whose participation in politics derives in the main from their desire to translate certain policy preferences into public policy. These people are not primarily oriented toward political jobs or privileges, though they may also seek these ends. Frequently, though not invariably, they are representatives of interest groups.

EMERGENCE OF ISSUE-ORIENTED PARTIES

The emergence of issue-oriented two-party systems in the United States is a recent development in American political parties. In the eighteenth and nineteenth centuries the Jeffersonians, early Republicans, and La Follette Progressives were primarily issue-oriented. However, Jacksonian Democracy, with its emphasis on spoils, and the Civil War, which resulted in a division of the electorate along lines only distantly related to the problems facing the electorate, produced political parties in most states and at the national level manned largely by job-oriented people. Job-oriented politics did not eliminate the policy differences between parties, because the sectional, ethnic, class, and religious differences among the people who voted Democratic as opposed to Republican by habit or tradition resulted in a fairly distinctive configuration of policy preferences among Republican as opposed to Democratic job-oriented politicians. However, the traditional composition of the parties was so broad (from Senator James Eastland of Mississippi to Vice-President Hubert Humphrey .in the Democratic party) and the policy concerns or interests of the job-oriented politicians so narrow that the programmatic or policy differences between the parties were minimized. The twentieth-century political norm was state and national political parties largely composed of people whose interest in politics was a product of their desire for jobs, contracts, or other personal perquisites of political power. Following World War II, programmatic or issue-oriented parties emerged in California, Michigan, Wisconsin, and Minnesota out of the increased issue-orientation occasioned by the New Deal and the war. Further, the Republican party at the national level appeared to be increasingly dominated by people whose central political purpose was the promotion of particular public policy ends. The Goldwater candidacy in 1964 was an effect of the Republican party's increased issue-orientation. The cause in the Republican party, as in the Democratic party, was the events surrounding the Great Depression and World War II.

Several aspects of this political development deserve attention: (1) the social and institutional factors that induced or precipitated the emergence of issue-oriented parties; (2) the relationships of issue-oriented parties to interest groups, public opinion, and government; and (3) the observable and measurable impact of issue-oriented parties on the performance of government and on society.

PROCESS OF POLITICAL TRANSFORMATION

There are several interesting and significant uniformities in the process by which the politics of Michigan, Wisconsin, and Minnesota were transformed from job-oriented to issue-oriented two-party systems in the years 1944-1948. These include: (1) strict civil service systems, which very nearly eliminated political patronage at both state and city levels; (2) the reduction of one party to an empty shell by repeated defeats at the polls; (3) the formation of well-organized interest groups with both the will and the means to seize control of the moribund political party; and

(4) the division of the electorate between the two major parties along lines related to mid-twentieth-century political, economic, and social problems.

The Michigan experience provides a useful case study of how each of these four conditions contributed to the development of two competitive programmatic parties.[1] Michigan's political parties had received little national attention until 1948, when G. Mennen ("Soapy") Williams, with the support of a coalition of liberal and labor leaders, won the Democratic nomination for governor over the opposition of old-line conservative Democrats. In the ensuing election, the state and the nation were warned that an "insidious" coalition of left-wing politicians was attempting to capture Michigan's government. Automobile manufacturers provided generous support to the Republicans as a counter to labor's support of the Democrats. Nevertheless, Williams won — although by a narrow margin.

In the following five gubernatorial contests Williams won re-election by ever-widening margins, and by 1958 virtually every statewide elective post was captured by Democrats. But it was not simply the electoral success of Williams and the Democrats in previously Republican Michigan that startled the nation; rather, it was the electoral success of a party headed by people concerned more with programs than with the traditional small change of politics. Neil Staebler, Democratic State Chairman during most of the 1948-1960 period, was a wealthy liberal who made a career of party politics out of devotion to liberal political goals. Similarly, labor leaders in the Democratic party did not seek contracts or jobs for union members but rather public policy oriented toward a redistribution of goods and opportunities through a progressive tax structure and generous welfare and education programs. There have been similarly motivated individuals in other parties at other times, but seldom have they so dominated a party.

Likewise, issue-oriented business and professional people who entered actively into partisan politics under the Republican label did not seek traditional forms of political preference. For example, George Romney, who was president of the American Motors Company before entering partisan politics, obviously had little economic advantage to gain by doing so. Rather, such men sought public policies that would encourage the growth of business enterprise in the state. Middle- and upper-management people in Ford, General Motors, Chrysler, and American Motors plunged into the political battle in order to realize public policy ends. The result was the creation in Michigan of two programmatic parties that offered the voters distinct alternatives of public policy.

The first seeds of Michigan's political transformation were

sown in the 1936 presidential and gubernatorial elections. Before 1936, Michigan's Democratic party was at least as conservative as the Republican party and was corrupt besides. Its primary *raison d'être* was to serve as a vehicle for political patronage when the Democrats won the presidential election, since before the Great Depression it had won few elections for state office. In addition, as is often the case with minority parties, its "tame" Democratic leaders received state and local patronage crumbs from the dominant Republicans; tame Democrats were useful to the Republicans as semiblind election officials and as sources of legislative votes when the Republican party was split. The Democratic voters were primarily the state's immigrant Irish and Eastern European Catholic population, who voted Democratic because it was the only political alternative to the Republican party.

The Republican party was the vehicle of the Anglo-Saxon Protestant settlers of the state. Prior to 1860 the early settlers were rather evenly split between the Democratic and the Republican parties, but the Civil War unified them in opposition to the South. The Irish, Polish, Italian, and other immigrants who settled in Michigan after the Civil War were therefore faced with a political as well as an economic world dominated by the native Anglo-Saxon Protestants. The weak Democratic party sought their votes and offered in return political jobs as well as welfare and law-enforcement practices designed to meet the needs of people in desperate economic straits. This meant help in finding apartments, buckets of coal and baskets of food, jobs as policemen, myopic enforcement of laws against betting on races, and support of demands for tax-supported school buses to transport children to parochial schools.

The 1936 election produced an irreversible transformation in the political division of Michigan's electorate. The less well-to-do of the state—including Protestant as well as Catholic, native-born as well as immigrant—flowed into the Democratic party, and the more well-to-do identified their interests with the Republican party. It might be noted that the Catholic-Protestant division of the electorate, which dated from the late nineteenth century, also tended to break along economic lines. However, the 1936 electoral division differed from that of the pre-1936 political world both in the sharpness of the income break between the parties and in the identification of the division with actual issues posed by the candidates.

In the 1936 presidential election Franklin Roosevelt played the role of champion of the downtrodden and, more specifically, of the workingmen as opposed to the "economic royalists." This is an example of how national events, great national conflicts, and compromises often give state parties their shape and determine their composition. Roosevelt decided that he needed a Democratic candidate for governor in Michigan who would support his policies and add strength to the ticket. He chose Frank Murphy to provide him with this needed ideological and electoral support and was able to force Murphy's nomination down the throats of old-guard Michigan Democrats by manipulating federal patronage. Murphy and Roosevelt both won landslide victories.

During the two stormy years that Murphy occupied the governor's office in Lansing, he bent every effort to facilitate the CIO's attempt to organize. Beginning with the National Recovery Act and culminating with the National Labor Relations Act, Roosevelt did everything in his power to encourage and promote collective bargaining and the recognition of unions by management. The terms of the National Labor Relations Act forced management to bargain with unions in good faith if a majority of the employees expressed a desire for such representation in an election supervised by the National Labor Relations Board. The motor industry bitterly resisted the efforts of unions to force organized bargaining, but Murphy supported the unions. When the unions resorted to sit-down (or sit-in) strikes, management insisted that Murphy use the National Guard to protect private property by ejecting the workers from the plants. Murphy refused, and, partly as a consequence, the motor companies finally agreed to bargain with the union leaders.

Murphy lost the 1938 election when the Democratic party split between its liberal and its conservative, or job-oriented, wings and the infant union movement was unable to provide much more than moral support. However, Murphy's brief tenure served to identify Michigan's Democratic party with the interests of labor and the "little man" in the minds of most Michigan voters. In succeeding elections from 1938 through 1946, the division of the electorate between the two parties along issue lines left the Republican party dominant for three reasons. First, labor was absorbed with problems of organization and with fighting internal Communist elements and had little time for state politics. (By 1948, these problems had been largely solved.) Second, conservative Democrats recaptured the party after 1938, and, as a consequence, the turnout of labor and liberal voters was quite low.

Third, in 1941 an event occurred that "good government" groups applauded. The League of Women Voters and allied organizations managed to persuade the Republican-dominated legislature to adopt a strict civil service law. If the Michigan Republicans who voted for the bill had looked beyond immediate self-interest, they would probably have reversed their decision, but they supported the law as a means of wrecking the Democratic party, which had maintained its existence up to that time primarily through jobs distributed to the party faithful by the elected superintendent of highways—a Democrat. In a sense, the Republicans were successful: Michigan's Democratic party as an organization virtually disappeared after 1941, and by 1946 it was powerless, despite the fact that most of the state's working people still thought of themselves as Democrats. Thus, the 1936 election and the New Deal at the national level facilitated a thorough realignment of Michigan political divisions, but its effectuation required leadership at the state level. The following study illustrates the role of effective leadership and the crucial influence of outside issue-oriented groups in utilizing political changes produced by great events to secure their desired policy ends.

The moribund state of the Democratic party in Michigan did not escape the attention of union leaders like Walter Reuther of the UAW or of liberals outside the labor movement like Democratic State Chairman Neil Staebler and G. Mennen Williams, who initially came together in the Americans for Democratic Action to work for Harry Truman's election in 1948 and to fight the efforts of left-wing elements to promote Henry Wallace's candidacy for President on the Progressive ticket. They compared notes on the condition of Michigan's Democratic party and agreed that it provided an opportunity for liberal and labor seizure of the party for the purpose of promoting their policy preferences. On March 13, 1948, a state CIO conference adopted the following resolution:

> Progressives and liberals within the Democratic party have often been outnumbered by conservative and reactionary elements. The PAC [Political Action Committee] is unanimous in its opinion that the best way of supporting liberalism within the Democratic party, to conform to the National CIO policy, and to serve the best interests of Michigan labor is to join the Democratic party. It is our objective in adopting this policy to remold the Democratic party into a real liberal and progressive political party which can be subscribed to by members of the CIO and other liberals. We therefore advise CIO members to become active precinct, ward, county, and congressional district leaders, and to attempt to become delegates to Democratic conventions.

Thus, a coalition of labor and liberal leaders joined hands in an attempt to obtain control of Michigan's Democratic party. In the subsequent election of precinct delegates to the six Democratic district conventions in Detroit, most labor and liberal candidates were successful. Because the city's foundering regular Democratic organization failed to contest the election in most of the precincts, the labor and liberal candidates dominated the Democratic district conventions and proceeded to elect their own delegates to the state Democratic convention. The representation of each district was proportionate to the votes cast for the Democratic candidate for secretary of state in the preceding election. Since Detroit had cast about half of the state votes for the Democratic candidate, the six city districts were allocated about half of the votes at the state convention. Consequently, the Detroit labor and liberal delegates were able to control the state convention with the help of sympathetic delegates from other cities and from the mining counties of the Upper Peninsula of Michigan.

After labor's success in capturing the Democratic party, it worked with unusual devotion for the election of Democrats in 1948 and thereafter. The unions both furnished manpower and contributed funds to the Democratic organization. As a result, the Detroit turnout and the Democratic vote swelled, leading to Democratic victories in gubernatorial elections from 1948 through 1960. In 1964, the Democratic party in Michigan controlled both houses of the state legislature and most of the statewide elective offices. However, victory at the polls would have been impossible without the participation of respected and respectable liberals outside the labor movement, whose names on the ballot and at the head of the Democratic organization blunted the charge that the party was the vehicle of labor unions. Without their participation, the Democratic party might have lost many moderate voters.

The Democratic liberals were more than a façade for a union-dominated political party; in fact, they controlled the Democratic state central committee in Michigan after 1948. Many labor leaders felt that the liberals discriminated against them in appointments to policy-making positions, but Walter Reuther and the UAW leadership were willing to remain in the political back seat because the liberals generally shared their policy preferences and because they realized that a labor-directed political party would have scant chance of electoral success.

In 1962, George Romney, president of the American Motors Company, won election as the Republican candidate for governor. Romney represented the moderate urban-based Republicans, who controlled the party at the state level during most of the period from 1952 through 1964. The moderate Republicans were as issue-oriented as the Democrats. They came largely from middle management in the motor companies and smaller business enterprises, and they had no more interest in political jobs and patronage than did the Democratic labor leaders. Rather, they were active in politics out of a desire to secure the "good society," meaning one that minimized governmental restraints on the individual and maintained a favorable business climate in Michigan.

The division of the Michigan electorate into two issue-oriented parties, offering the voters rather distinct alternatives in terms of candidates and public policy, did not result in bitter political battles that endangered democratic political institutions. The reason was that the Romneys of the motor companies and the Reuthers of the labor unions were acquainted with one another and respected one another's ability and point of view. Further, the requirements of electoral strategy in Michigan tended to keep the parties fairly close together, for experience had proved to Republican leaders that if they moved too far to the political right, they forfeited any chance of electoral victory.

The process by which Wisconsin's and Minnesota's political parties were transformed into competitive programmatic parties was similar to that in Michigan. In both states, the enactment of strict civil service laws rid the parties of men who made their living from day-to-day political activity. In both states the Democratic party was an empty shell, although potentially a large organism because of the political popularity of Franklin Roosevelt and his New Deal, and in both states the Democratic party was seized in the 1940's by liberal and labor coalitions.

CHARACTERISTICS AND GOALS

After the 1940's the distinctive attribute of people in politics in Michigan, Wisconsin, and Minnesota was their disdain for jobs and contracts. Attractive and aggressive women,[2] college professors, wealthy liberals, and union leaders gravitated into the Democratic party. Businessmen, middle-management and some upper-management corporation employees, professional people, and recruits from the League of Women Voters were to be found in the Republican party. Both parties also attracted attorneys and others who had an interest in jobs and the other more traditional perquisites of political power, but they generally held subordinate party positions.

These people were in politics from many motives, but they professed a concern for good government and the good society. They differed widely on the definition of these goals. Of course, some were after power for its own sake, but they rationalized this goal in policy terms. The domination of both parties by issue-oriented people with differing policy preferences resulted in parties that met one another head-on in terms of public policy. The Democratic parties in all three states were committed to egalitarian objectives that served the self-interest of their low-income adherents, while the Republican parties identified themselves with the individualistic values of the frontier—which, incidentally, corresponded nicely to the self-interest of their middle-class adherents, because frontier values tended to associate poverty with laziness and immorality and thus discredited equalitarian taxes and governmental programs.

The role of women in issue-oriented politics is a particularly interesting phenomenon. Their presence in large numbers is at least partially due to the absence of job-oriented men. Strict civil service laws eliminate opportunities to make a living out of politics; therefore, unless men are independently wealthy or in a profession that relates political activity to success, such as the law, they must treat politics as an avocation. Middle-class women, though, have time to devote to politics and also find that it provides opportunities absent in other professions where competition with men is keener. Politics is often a part-time occupation, hence difficult for busy men but ideal for some mothers whose domestic responsibilities allow time for outside activities.

The predilection of issue-oriented middle-class women for politics of both the extreme left and the extreme right also deserves attention.[3] A possible reason for the enlistment of women in extreme politics is the relative narrowness of their associations with groups and individuals. If a man becomes interested in extreme politics, his views are likely to be challenged by both his associates at work and his neighborhood friends. In addition, men commonly have histories of associations that cross class, religious, and other lines through their military service as well as in their careers. Typically, women have a less variegated history of friendship and associations, and when they acquire extreme political views, they are less likely to have their ideas challenged by friends or experience.

The tendency of issue-oriented women to pursue narrowly defined political objectives is also evident within more moderate political groupings. For example, in Lexington, Kentucky, one respected woman who is active in Democratic politics devotes her entire attention to the need for more generous state and local support of programs designed to provide aid to handicapped children. One of the woman's children is mentally retarded. Another female political activist in Lexington has a child with cerebral palsy, and in her opinion all political and governmental problems begin and end with the need for expanded governmental programs designed to prevent cerebral palsy or to help its victims. Returning to the issue-oriented political parties in Michigan, Wisconsin, and Minnesota, perhaps the most typical example of their programmatic character was the 1956 *Michigan Declaration,* a statement of Democratic party principle prepared with the help of professors at the state universities. The *Declaration* was a twentieth-century liberal document that emphasized an egalitarian approach to the problems of society and the importance of government in serving these egalitarian objectives. In part, the *Declaration* held that:

> So long as one human being is hungry and we can feed him and do not, so long as one person is naked and we can clothe him and do not, so long as one person is sick and we can minister to him and do not, so long as one worker or farmer is deprived of a just living and we can remedy it and do not, so long as one person is unwillingly illiterate and we can educate him and do not, so long as one nation is subjugated by another against its will and we can work for freedom and do not, the American task is not done.

Typical of the Republican position on issues was the statement of Representative Van Peursem, former Speaker of the Michigan House of Representatives, who maintained that "good government is by definition the least government possible commensurate with the needs of domestic tranquillity and provisions for the security of the nation from external aggression. . . . big government always results in tyranny no matter how well-intentioned." Michigan Republicans such as Van Peursem do not advocate a return to the nineteenth century, but they seek to minimize governmental and other controls over the individual and attempt to maximize opportunities for individual accomplishment and self-realization. Frequently, this includes support for public education, but it also involves adamant opposition to so-called "handout" welfare legislation and bills designed to limit the freedom of the individual to use his property as he wishes.

RELATIONSHIP TO PUBLIC OPINION

Most mid-twentieth-century political scientists relate an informed electorate which chooses from among alternatives to the existence of issue-oriented political parties, a relationship which runs both ways. According to political party theory, parties in a democracy are assigned the task of providing the people with distinct alternatives in the form of candidates and platforms. In the process of seeking the election of their candidates, parties inform the electorate about current problems and challenges and offer competing solutions. Thus informed, citizens are able to cast meaningful ballots that, in broad terms, determine the nature of their society.[4]

A minority of political scientists and perhaps a majority of journalists have expressed reservations about the desirability of issue-oriented parties in the United States.[5] They grant that such parties make politics more meaningful and government more responsive to majority rule. But they point out that one reason American democracy has been successful is that the political parties have commonly "knitted up" rather than "torn out" seams in the social fabric. The principal point made by those who disapprove of the creation of issue-oriented parties is that democracy works only when the minority in an election does not lose too much. If the parties provide alternatives that are too widely separated, the theory goes, the losers are likely to "man the barricades" out of fear that they will lose their property and their liberties. History indicates that when the interests of community groups tend to cleave on many issues or when a divisive issue, such as slavery, overshadows all others, civil strife is likely to occur.

A plausible third theory is that political parties have little to do with either informing or influencing the public, that the nature of a party system is an effect of public opinion rather than a cause. According to this conceptualization of the political world, an issue-oriented two-party system works quite well where strong consensual bonds unite the individuals in the society.

For example, the British Labour and Conservative parties provide voters with distinct alternatives in terms of public policy. However, when the Labour party won the 1945 election, property owners did not man the barricades despite wide differences between the two parties on the issues of nationalization of industry and medicine. Similarly, when the Conservatives returned to power in 1951, workingmen did not dash for the Tower of London brandishing muskets and pitchforks. Rational behavior prevailed in both cases, it seems, because most Britishers feel themselves part of a community in which the needs of one are felt by all and also because they believe in the importance of the "rules of the political game" and will do much to protect today's minority, including its right to try to become tomorrow's majority. Most of Britain's well-to-do citizens genuinely felt in 1945 that the good society for which they had been fighting required allotting a fairer share of goods and opportunities to the less prosperous.

Similarly, most British workers would make their employers managers of socialized industries. In part, this consensual bond was a product of the shared suffering of World War II. In larger part, perhaps, it was a result of a stable constitutional system that had successfully accommodated itself to profound social, economic, and political change. On the other hand, no such consensual bond exists between groups in France. Prior to World War II, the cry of the French rightists was "Better Hitler than Blum."[6] The fragmented political parties reflected the widely differing popular demands and were virtually at war with one another. Before General de Gaulle took office, there were many highly ideological political parties and sharp divisions between the rich and the poor, the property owners and the working class, the farmers and the residents of cities.

The process by which issue-oriented parties have emerged in the United States, and the results therefrom, indicate that there is some truth in all three theories of the nature and effect of issue-oriented parties on public opinion.

There is little question but that the emergence of issue-oriented parties in Michigan, Wisconsin, and Minnesota was the result of certain institutional and social changes, among them the development of a broader consensus concerning the nature of the good society. Surprisingly, this broader consensus was due partly to the organization of labor unions, whose leaders regularly interacted with the managers of industry in collective bargaining. In the motor industry, at least, these meetings engendered a new understanding and sense of community between leaders on both sides. In 1964, for example, one reason that Michigan's Governor Romney did not support Barry Goldwater in the presidential election campaign was that he believed Goldwater's views to be hostile to social security and labor unions.

It is also true that issue-oriented political parties, once created, influence and shape the public opinion from which they emerge. They provide condidates and advocate public policies that offer voters genuine alternatives and meaningful ballots. They also disturb the individuals who feel themselves outside the consensus from which the parties arose. These alienated souls consider issue-oriented parties to be a rash on a sick society and charge that the present political system is blind to key needs or dangers, whether Communism or fluoridation. There is some reason to believe that the political climate of states with issue-oriented parties has been particularly congenial to the growth of the John Birch Society, although its growth in states such as Texas indicates that it can also prosper in job-oriented states.

However, none of the above theories accounts for one important aspect of the development of two-party issue-oriented politics—the fact that a fairly equal division of the electorate along lines related to twentieth-century issues has been a vital precondition of the emergence of an issue-oriented two-party system. It would seem that job-oriented parties contain within them the seeds of their own destruction; that, essentially, they are poles that attract divergent elements on contemporary issues; and that, when these elements become sufficiently cohesive, they seize control of the parties.

As will be seen in subsequent chapters, however, an equally good argument might be made that a two-party system is dysfunctional if its object is to maintain issue-oriented divisions of the electorate. Political parties tend to keep alive old issues that have little or no bearing on current problems. For obvious reasons they continue to peddle wares that have sold well in the past. Equally important, the old issues brought the party together in the first place. A new issue endangers the existing unity of the party and invariably involves the loss of some of its constituents. Therefore, before adopting a position on a new issue, party leaders carefully weigh the probable gain of new groups against the possible loss of loyal adherents. Witness, for example, the decades during which the Republicans waved the bloody shirt of the rebellion and, for another, the continued tendency of Democrats to run against Herbert Hoover and the 1929 depression.

It is possible that a bifactional one-party system is more likely to reflect contemporary divisions over issues. As will be seen in Chapter Five, most one-party states, such as Louisiana and the Dakotas, date their party allegiance from near-unanimous support of or opposition to the secession of the Confederacy from the Union. Thereafter, the division of the electorate between candidates on the single-party ticket tended to be related to contemporary issues rather than to the old issue of the Civil War on which almost everyone was agreed. Further, since there were no institutionalized groups to keep alive the old issues, any new divisions would also be caused by specific problems facing the electorate.

In summary, the recent development of issue-oriented parties in a few states has followed the division of the electorate along lines related to twentieth-century issues and has been accompanied by the strengthening of the consensual bond among all elements of the society. If the consensual bond were not strengthened by increased interaction between groups, the electorate would probably divide in many directions and a fragmented party system would result, as has happened in states of the Deep South. For example, in Mississippi and Florida, it is not uncommon for five or more candidates to contend for the Democratic nomination for governor. As a result of two-party issue-oriented politics, however, the electorate is provided with meaningful choices and is thus enabled to vote in terms of informed self-interest modified by a sense of community.

RELATIONSHIP TO INTEREST GROUPS

One striking departure of issue-oriented American parties from traditional forms is their tendency to attract interest groups. In theory, parties stand between interest groups, which seek particularistic ends, and government, which must mediate disputes and pursue policies that will promote the general welfare. The parties, then, aggregate and synthesize the separate goals of interest groups into programs which they hope will attract a majority of votes in an election. If a party wins the election, it then has a mandate to translate its creative synthesis of the interest group demands into public policies that will help solve group disputes and realize the general welfare.

In Michigan, however, the United Auto Workers has become part of the Democratic party, and the motor companies have in a sense become part of the Republican party, suggesting the alarming possibility that the political parties and then the government may become instruments of those particular interest groups. Nothing of the sort has actually happened. No interest group has the power to win an election independent of other groups. Consequently, the United Auto Workers has had to ally itself with liberals and with job-oriented politicians. In the process, it has stopped acting as an interest group seeking particularistic ends and has adopted many of the characteristics of a political party, seeking not only bread and butter but also a better world for its members. This "better world" means good schools, parks, and mental institutions and generous social security and welfare programs for all citizens. Further, it advocates tax programs that will attract industry to the state, for it wants full employment.

The motor companies in the Republican party also find it necessary to accommodate to the wide variety of interests associated with that party and to the practical demands of winning elections. Therefore, the Fords and Romneys do not seek only profits; they seek also a prosperous state. A consensus has developed in Michigan concerning some of the elements essential to a prosperous state, including good schools as well as good highways, efficient and effective services as well as a favorable business climate.

In some ways, the entrance of interest groups into active

membership in political parties facilitates the development of a closer consensual bond in society. So long as interest groups stand outside parties, they feel free to make the most extreme and self-seeking demands on the parties and government. However, once inside the parties, they are forced to think in broader terms. More precisely, when interest group leaders are members of political parties, they must actively participate in the aggregative and synthesizing functions of the parties. This invariably affects the policies of the interest groups and reduces the policy differences between the interest groups and the parties.

EFFECT ON GOVERNMENT PERFORMANCE

According to their advocates, issue-oriented political parties are more likely than job-oriented parties to provide honest, responsible, and responsive government. If the performance in office of the issue-oriented parties of Michigan, Wisconsin, and Minnesota is any guide, there is some truth to this assertion. All impressionistic evidence indicates that the governments of the three states are manned by people who are almost painfully honest. There are few scandals of the kind that periodically explode in job-oriented party states such as Indiana, Illinois, and Massachusetts. This is not too surprising, because most of the elected officials in issue-oriented states are there out of concern for issues rather than a desire for material perquisites of power.

Perhaps most important, evidence indicates that there is a measurable difference in the performance of government in states with issue-oriented parties as opposed to states with job-oriented parties. In a study of Midwest politics[7] the author compared the welfare and education expenditure efforts of Ohio, Indiana, and Illinois (all job-oriented states) with those of Michigan, Wisconsin, and Minnesota (see Table X in Chapter Four). In every instance the states with issue-oriented parties made greater expenditure efforts than did the states with job-oriented parties. The implication, of course, is that issue-oriented parties are more responsive to the majority demands for a larger share of society's goods and opportunities.

One check upon the responsiveness of issue-oriented parties in the Midwest was their legislatures. In each of the states the legislature was dominated by less urban, conservative interests, due to malapportionment, while the governor was elected in large part by more urban and more liberal groups. One result was that the governor's programs were frequently blocked. Another result was the steady strengthening of the governorship, for the legislature played a purely negative role while the governor was called upon to provide blueprints for the state's efforts to meet its problems. Consequently, the legislature simply reacted to the governor's initiatives, and the programs of state government thus tended to be the governor's programs, albeit often modified or curtailed by the legislature. Reapportionment in Michigan on a one-man, one-vote basis resulted in the election in 1964 of a Democratic-controlled legislature and a Republican governor. Potential party conflicts did not materialize and the legislature cooperated closely with the governor in 1965, which suggests that equitable reapportionment may eliminate this check upon the responsiveness of issue-oriented parties.

CONCLUSIONS

In summary, it can be said that two-party issue-oriented state politics does result in substantial, measurable differences in the character and performance of government. The differences tend to be those predicted by students of government — more honest, more responsive, and more responsible government. The danger that issue-oriented politics might produce irreconcilable party differences has not materialized at the state level. One reason seems to be that in Michigan, Minnesota, and Wisconsin a consensual bond inhibits the development of wide gulfs between the parties. Another reason is that issue-oriented politicians, once elected, gravitate toward the political middle out of a desire to assure re-election; in other words, they assume some of the characteristics of job-oriented political figures.

At present, the most important question is whether issue-oriented national politics results in socially harmful divisions of opinion. One tentative explanation of the relatively wider divisions at the national than at the state level as a consequence of issue-oriented politics is that the consensual bonds of society are much looser nationally; for example, there is no consensual bond between the whites of the Deep South and the nation's Negroes.

CHAPTER FOUR

Two-Party
Job-Oriented Politics

Two competitive, typically job-oriented parties have held sway in the nation and in most of the states since the era of Andrew Jackson. In most one-party states the orientation has also been toward jobs. The distinguishing characteristic of a job-oriented system is that the people who participate in politics on a day-to-day basis do so out of a desire for jobs, contracts, or other personal gains rather than because of a concern for public policy.

In political parlance, the result is election battles between the "ins" and the "outs." The ins are people who have the jobs and contracts and want to keep them. The outs are the lean and hungry individuals who want the jobs and contracts. The professional political boss is equivalent to a corporation manager. He is employed by the ins and the outs to develop and maintain an effective organizational means of obtaining the votes necessary for political victory. Interest groups, concerned only with issues, operate outside job-oriented parties; they attempt to influence individual officeholders and candidates of both parties. The classic statement of the role of interest groups in a job-oriented political system was the formula followed by Samuel Gompers, the long-time AFL president: "Reward your friends and punish your enemies."

JOB-ORIENTED POLITICS IN KENTUCKY

Kentucky is an example of a state with job-oriented political parties.[1] It is a two-party state, but the Democrats win most elections. Almost all state employees receive their jobs through the good offices of political leaders. When administrations change, employees must scurry to secure the support of the new political leaders. In the personnel office, any job application not accompanied by a recommendation from the administration's county political leader is usually discarded. Governor Bert T. Combs (1959-1963) installed a civil service system, but political considerations remained significant. Similarly, contracts are let on a partially political basis.

It is interesting to follow the process by which a newly elected governor uses his job and contract power to build an effective political organization. He invariably enjoys a great deal of political power by virtue of these emoluments of government that he can distribute to grateful friends and supporters.

After election, one of the first acts of an incumbent governor in Kentucky is to designate an "administration man" in each county of the state. Typical of the procedure followed was Governor Earl Clements' appointment in 1947 of Bill Simpson as administration man in Nelson County, where Simpson had worked as Clements' campaign manager. Clements had asked Simpson to serve as a campaign manager because Simpson, a successful and respected businessman who owned an automobile agency and a service station, wielded considerable influence in the community. Simpson had accepted the job because he desired the position of county administration man. When Clements carried Nelson County in both the primary and the general elections, therefore, Simpson had a legitimate claim on the job.

No newspaper announcement of Simpson's appointment was made because the post is neither a formal governmental nor a party position. Rather, it is an informal working relationship between the governor and the individual. The following portion of a telephone call from Clements to Simpson after the election illustrates this informality:

> Bill, you're pretty well acquainted with the people in Nelson County—those who were for me in the election and those who were "agin" me. I wish you'd take care of

all the good people who worked for me and try to do something about those who fought me. Bill, I've told the people in personnel and the highway department that no one should be hired from Nelson County without your O.K. Further, the manager at the State Highway Garage in Bardstown knows that you're the boss. I'll sure be grateful to you, Bill, if you'll do this job for me.

Simpson paused just long enough to observe the amenities, then replied, "Governor, I thank you for your confidence and I can assure you that I'll do everything possible to build up a good organization here in Nelson County."

After exchanging conventional pleasantries, the conversation was terminated, and Simpson leaned back in his swivel chair, looked out at the busy mechanics in his garage, and allowed a happy grin to crease his usually solemn face. He reached for the telephone, called three or four of his cronies, opened the bottom desk drawer and removed a bottle of good Nelson County bourbon, told his secretary to get some paper cups, and made ready for a celebration. Simpson's delight at becoming Clements' administration man was because of the power that accompanied the appointment and the various personal and economic rewards that ordinarily accompany the power.

After the telephone call in 1947 and until "Happy" Chandler's election as governor in 1955, Simpson controlled the distribution of hundreds of jobs, had a voice in the awarding of business contracts, and had an important if not a controlling voice in public policy as it affected Nelson County. Any person employed by the State Highway Garage in Bardstown, the county seat, held his job through the good offices and at the pleasure of Bill Simpson. In addition, county residents seeking employment in the various state government departments in Frankfort found it necessary to acquire Simpson's recommendation. Any vendor, supply house, or construction company located in Nelson County and doing business with the state found it expedient to secure Simpson's endorsement of its products or services. Theoretically, the Division of Purchases in the Department of Finance awarded contracts on the basis of the lowest and best bid; however, "lowest and best" is a formula open to interpretation, and if a buyer wanted to insure that a particular vendor received a given order, he had only to insert in the order a specification involving what might be a very minor but nevertheless unique quality of the product offered only by that particular vendor.

Simpson's power and prerogatives in the realm of public policy included such matters as the location and direction of new state highways. For example, Theodore Shehan wanted the county road that skirted his farm classified as a state highway and black-topped. The county road was inadequately maintained and quite dusty, and Mrs. Shehan complained bitterly about the gritty layer of dirt that blanketed the furniture, particularly during the dry dog days of August. Shehan was a prosperous farmer who owned several hundred acres of fertile bluegrass land and who had helped organize and manage a successful cooperative tobacco warehouse in Bloomfield. More to the point, he was a loyal Democrat who had always worked for Democratic candidates in general elections; he took great pride in his ability to deliver about one hundred votes from his precinct and to predict his precinct's vote within one or two ballots. In 1947, Shehan worked with Simpson for Clements' nomination as the Democratic gubernatorial candidate and for his election in November. The expected Clements pluralities were registered in Shehan's precinct. After Simpson was appointed administration man, Shehan approached him about the highway, marshaling as many arguments as an essentially weak case would support. Although the dusty road served only about thirty families, the Highway Department apparently discovered that the one hundred votes controlled by Shehan outweighed engineering and service arguments, and the road was subsequently incorporated into the state highway system. Thereafter, Mrs. Shehan was able to relax on a clean and shaded porch on hot August days, and Simpson had won Shehan's support for at least the next election.[2]

Other examples of an administration man's possible actions include directing the "political curves" on state and national highways to depart insanely from their logical paths in order to preserve the front yard of a political friend and intervening to rescind or postpone a draft notice.

Not surprisingly, Simpson was able to construct an effective political machine in Nelson County with his patronage powers. The employees at the State Highway Garage in Bardstown were always responsive to Simpson's requests for campaign contributions or campaign work, and the recipients of contracts or other services from Simpson were equally eager to demonstrate their gratitude through generous campaign contributions or by delivering their precincts for administration candidates.

The impression derived from Simpson's conversation was that his central reason for taking part in political activities was his strong sense of citizen responsibility—his belief that it is a businessman's duty to devote a portion of his time to public service. Perhaps it is not overly ungenerous, however, to suggest that he had other motives also, for, as mentioned earlier, his work gained him numerous psychic and material returns. For example, as a consequence of the political machine he controlled, Simpson was elected mayor of Bardstown and was able to secure the election of Judge Beeler to the post of county judge, the most important administrative post in the area. Also flowing from his political power at the state, county, and city levels was a stream of business for his automobile agency and service station. In case of a wreck, the state police, sheriff's deputies, or city police would call Simpson's garage for wrecker service. Similarly, when the state purchased automobiles, Simpson often shared generously in the sales, for the auto company whose bid was adjudged the "lowest and best" frequently proved to be a manufacturer from whom Simpson held a dealership. If so, the manufacturer asked state officials to name the ten dealers from whom they would prefer to purchase, say, five cars each; Simpson's name was invariably included among the preferred dealers. Furthermore, the manufacturer might not sell the automobiles directly to the state but might instead deliver all fifty cars to Simpson's garage. Simpson then would inform the Highway Department that the cars were available, whereupon Department employees would be dispatched to take possession. Simpson would receive $50 for each car sold and $50 for each delivered. In this example, each of the nine dealers who never saw the five automobiles they sold to the state would receive $250, while Simpson would receive $250 for the five cars sold plus $2500 for the fifty cars delivered by him to the state.

Thus, in Nelson County a political machine was built, based primarily upon jobs, contracts, and a desire for power and profit. Next we shall explore the way this kind of political machine functioned and the public policy effects that resulted from it.

RELATIONSHIP TO PUBLIC OPINION

There would seem to be a relationship between job-oriented politics and the division of the electorate between the parties along lines unrelated to contemporary issues and problems.[3] It is impossible to state without qualification that there is a cause-and-effect relationship between these two political conditions, but the two do seem to reinforce each other. In states such as Kentucky, Indiana, Illinois, Missouri, West Virginia, Maryland, and Ohio, the division of the electorate between the Democratic and Republican parties is in large part a product of the Civil War. In each of the states, much of the support received by Democratic and Republican candidates in the 1960's rose out of the events of the 1860's. In all these states, the people living in formerly

Copperhead or pro-Southern sections tended to find the arguments of Democratic candidates in the 1960's peculiarly persuasive. Similarly, the Unionist strongholds of the 1860's tended
to be Republican strongholds in the 1960's unless they contained
mass-production industries or coal mines, in which case the
Great Depression of the 1930's took precedence in influencing
voting behavior in a Democratic direction.

As was pointed out in *Politics in the Border States,*

> people receive their political preconceptions from their
> parents in the same fashion as all prejudices are trans-
> mitted from father to son. A political bias once formed,
> like a religious affiliation, is difficult to shake. Very occa-
> sionally, however, some earthshaking event occurs which
> changes the political environment sufficiently to induce
> large numbers of people to change their political affiliations.
> At the same time, however, the political convictions of the
> great majority of the population remain unaffected.[4]

(The Negro civil rights movement in the mid-twentieth century
may prove to have been the "earthshaking event" of that generation which changed political affiliations.) The fact remains, though,
that the causative factors behind the votes of millions of people
in the 1960's were the events of the Civil War or the Great Depression.

Wherever voting is so unrelated to the problems that currently face society, the people who are active in day-to-day politics
tend to be those who seek some direct material return from their
political activity, such as jobs or contracts. After all, if politics is
divorced from the broad issues of the day and, consequently, if
government makes little or no impact on people's lives outside of
jobs, blacktopping roads, and immigration visas for relatives,
then what other motivation exists for political participation? In
low-income states the job-oriented political system does generate
a great deal of interest in politics on the part of the citizenry. In
Kentucky, politics is discussed on virtually every street corner.
However, it is seldom a discussion of issues; rather, the contro-
versies revolve around personalities and jobs.

In more well-to-do urbanized states, such as Ohio or Massachusetts, issueless politics induces a rather general indifference
toward politics and results in thousands of "alienated voters."
People in urbanized states do not show the same interest in
personalities, such as "Happy" Chandler, that may be found in
low-income rural states. Further, since the family unit is less
cohesive in an urban area, the concern with political jobs stops

at the doorstep of the immediate family concerned, whereas in rural areas a political job for one individual may excite the interest and influence the votes of scores of cousins and aunts and uncles. In Kentucky, the campaign for the election of Wix Unthank as county judge of Harlan County stimulated intense interest on the part of Unthank's clan and also his wife's clan, both of which number in the hundreds.

In both low-income and high-income job-oriented, two-party states, however, the effect on public opinion of issueless politics is similar. There is seldom any discernible relationship between the economic self-interest of the electorate (in terms of broad issues as opposed to political jobs) and their balloting. Since there is rarely any public policy impact on the voter as a result of election victories or defeats, the voter seldom thinks in terms of public policy when he casts his ballot. Rather, his attention tends to be diverted from issues to relatively irrelevant aspects of the political campaign, such as the personalities, appearance, ethnic backgrounds, and religious preferences of candidates. On occasion, of course, there is a positive relationship rather than a dichotomy between these less relevant aspects and the voter's positions on issues, but personalities, religious preferences, and ethnic backgrounds are more often than not used to obscure the relationship rather than to subject it to intelligent scrutiny. The consequent policy illiteracy of the voters results in votes cast for a "Happy" Chandler of Kentucky because "he is a smart son of a bitch," or for John Bricker of Ohio "because he looks like a senator."

The reinforcing quality of job-oriented politics and a partisan division of the electorate along lines unrelated to contemporary problems is apparent from the foregoing description of the effect of the system on public opinion. Job-oriented politicians retain control because no one else is terribly concerned with politics. Few people associate politics with issues because they seldom see any relation between politics and their welfare. And so long as government's impact on their lives is unrelated to broad issues, they find little reason to change political affiliations. Thus, people who vote Democratic or Republican for reasons related to the Civil War continue to vote in this fashion because they are rarely if ever offered another reason for casting their vote. In short, politics is issueless and rather fruitless for all save the people who want jobs or contracts.

Job-oriented politicians rarely provide the electorate either with solutions or with information that would enable them to arrive at majority decisions concerning the kinds of solutions they prefer to the problems they face. Moreover, in those relatively rare instances when a deviant politician emerges who does formulate a program, there are no institutionalized means (party organizations, newspapers, labor unions) by which he can convey it to the electorate.

RELATIONSHIP TO INTEREST GROUPS

Not surprisingly, interest groups operate outside the political parties in two-party job-oriented states, since they seldom want jobs or contracts for their members but are concerned with public policy as it affects their members. Thus, an interest group rarely if ever becomes part of a job-oriented political party. Rather, it attempts to influence public policy through lobbying activities in the legislative, executive, and judicial branches of government.

A good example of the relation between an interest group and a job-oriented political party is the association between the Democrats in West Virginia and the United Mine Workers. In the 1956 campaign, Bill Blizzard, president of the local UMW district, received a telephone call from the Democratic party's publicity chairman, who requested a list of UMW members for the purpose of circulating Democratic campaign propaganda. Blizzard replied, "Why didn't you vote with us at the last Unemployment Compensation Board meeting?" At the meeting in question, some UMW members lost their plea for unemployment compensation during a strike, which, they had complained, was in fact a lockout. After delivering a tirade to the Democratic official, Blizzard flatly refused to provide him with the list, suggesting instead that the official send his propaganda to UMW headquarters where it might or might not be mailed to the members.

The exchange between Blizzard and the Democrat illustrates the nature of the relationship between the union and the Democratic party as well as the position of pressure groups vis-à-vis job-oriented political parties. The UMW ordinarily supported Democratic party candidates in West Virginia dating from Franklin Roosevelt and the New Deal, but it had never been a part of the party. Indeed, it exerted unusual efforts to keep its officials out of political party activity.

On occasion, Blizzard disapproved of Democratic party nominees. In 1942, for example, Matthew M. Neely, long-time Democratic leader in West Virginia, sought election to the United States Senate about midway in his term as governor of the state. Blizzard and the United Mine Workers withheld their support from Neely, who was subsequently defeated. Blizzard explained the UMW's action as follows: "Old Matt was getting a 'leetle' bit

big for his britches. During the entire campaign he didn't come
to us once for help or advice. Therefore, we just went fishing on
election day."[5] Translated, Blizzard's "go fishing" instructions
to union leaders meant "Do not get out the miner vote." This
was his only means of forcing Democrats to conform to UMW
policy preferences, for a substantial vote by the miners usually
resulted in a substantial Democratic victory. If this were not the
case, few Democratic politicians would have exerted themselves
very vigorously in support of UMW policies, for they were primarily concerned with the jobs and contracts obtainable through
control of government. For instance, Homer Hanna, the leader of
the party, was an insurance agent from whom the state purchased
90 per cent of its insurance coverage; the governor's father was
a salesman for a large liquor company and received a salary of
about $30,000 a year for selling liquor to state-owned liquor
stores.

This was not a party that Blizzard cared to enter. Rather,
he attempted to maintain cordial relations with Republican as
well as Democratic leaders. For example, in the 1950's, when
Republican State Chairman Walter Hallanan was involved in a
factional feud within the Republican party, he could usually
rely on the coal counties to vote substantial pluralities for his
candidates in Republican primaries. Most of Hallanan's support
in these predominantly Democratic counties emanated from the
local Republican leaders, who were dependent upon him for jobs
and campaign funds. However, Hallanan also relied upon the
good graces of Bill Blizzard for the vote his candidates received
in Republican primaries. For example, the union people "looked
the other way" when the Hallanan Republicans counted the
ballots. In return, Hallanan often turned a sympathetic ear to
Blizzard's suggestions about candidates and policies. In fact,
Hallanan's factional Republican enemies accused him of helping
the UMW and the Democrats to stab conservative Republicans
in the back.[6]

Historically, most interest groups have adopted similar
stands relative to political parties. Frequently their interests are
better served by one party than the other because their members
traditionally vote for that party. Although interest groups have
rarely entered a party, they have attempted to influence its platform and selection of candidates by implied or explicit threats
to "go fishing" on election day.

Interest groups have also tried to keep at least a toehold in
the other party so that its victory would not bar the groups'
access to officeholders. Indeed, securing such access is the main
objective of interest group leaders in a job-oriented political

system. The degree of access after election is always strongly influenced by the quantity and timeliness of the interest group's support and by the politician's calculation of its importance in the next election. In such politics, virtually all interest groups have some measure of access, and there is an effort by politicians to please everyone. Some groups are often able to push their particularistic goals very far indeed — farther than under issue-oriented politics, which tends to dilute their particularism, as was pointed out in Chapter Three.

EFFECT ON GOVERNMENT PERFORMANCE

The myth is widely accepted by political scientists that honest, responsible, and responsive government is very difficult if not impossible without two-party competition. The rationale behind the myth is that the leaders of the majority party must be responsive to the electorate or they will be voted out of office. On the other hand, the minority party must criticize the performance of the majority party and offer policy alternatives to the electorate if it is to achieve majority party status.

The myth is not without some substance. The evidence presented in Chapter Two showed that there is a measurable distinction in terms of government performance between states in which the electorate is rather evenly divided between the two parties and states in which one party wins with little or no competition. The distinction was that two-party states tend to be more responsive to the policy preferences of the numerous low-income people than are one-party states.

However, analyses of the various kinds of two-party competition establish fairly clearly that in states with job-oriented competition, the measurable responsiveness of government to the wishes of the electorate is not much more visible than in one-party states and is perhaps less pronounced than in one-party bifactional states. Table IX revealed that the states in which people spent the smallest part of their income on public services tended to be two-party job-oriented states where the partisan division of the electorate was along lines unrelated to contemporary problems.

Perhaps the most dramatic evidence of the Scrooge-like character of two-party job-oriented states is provided by comparing the issue-oriented two-party states of Michigan, Wisconsin, and Minnesota with the job-oriented two-party states of Ohio, Indiana, and Illinois in terms of the effort devoted to governmental programs that reallocate goods and opportunities. Table X reveals that in every instance the three issue-oriented states spent more relative to per capita income than the three job-oriented states

TABLE X

Comparative Expenditures on Governmental Programs Plus Demographic and Political Data for Six Midwest States

	Two-party competition score, 1946–1958	*Total effort* Per cent of per capita income collected as per capita state and local tax revenue, 1959[a]	*Welfare effort* Per cent of per capita income used for per capita welfare expenditures (less federal), 1959[b]	*Education effort* Per cent of 1959 per capita income used for education expenditures per pupil in ADA, 1959–1960[c]	Per capita income, 1959[a]	Per cent urban residents, 1960[d]	Per cent rural-farm residents, 1960[d]
Job-oriented two-party states							
Ohio	77	6.9	0.55	15.7	$2328	73.4	5.4
Indiana	83	8.0	0.34	16.9	2102	62.4	10.4
Illinois	89	6.7	0.45	15.4	2610	80.7	5.6
Issue-oriented two-party states							
Minnesota	*	10.3	0.76	20.6	1962	62.2	17.2
Wisconsin	73	9.3	0.62	18.2	2116	63.8	14.0
Michigan	80	8.7	0.60	18.9	2253	73.4	5.6

[a] U.S. Bureau of the Census. *Statistical Abstract of the United States, 1961.*

[b] U.S. Department of Commerce. Bureau of the Census. *Governmental Finances in 1959.*

[c] Research Division. National Education Association. *Rankings of the States, 1960.*

[d] U.S. Bureau of the Census. *County and City Data Book, 1962.*

* No competition score because Minnesota's legislative elections are nonpartisan.

SOURCE: John H. Fenton. *Midwest Politics* (New York: Holt, Rinehart & Winston, Inc., 1966). p. 230.

on the given public services and on the total costs of government. The comparative demographic data show that the six states do not differ substantially in per capita income or in urban-rural divisions. Further, the six states are in the same geographic and cultural area—the Midwest. Thus, the evidence would seem to indicate that the unresponsive character of the governments of the job-oriented states is traceable to the types of parties and to the divisions of the electorate along lines unrelated to contemporary problems.

Some political scientists maintain that this evidence of limited expenditure provides an excellent argument in favor of job-oriented politics. Those who prefer a government that minimizes its activities and does little to change the given allocation of power, goods, and opportunities would certainly prefer the politics of Kentucky. On the other hand, those who entertain a more positive concept of government, viewing it as a means of cleansing society of social and economic wrongs, would certainly prefer an issue-oriented politics, such as Michigan's.

CONCLUSIONS

The argument of this chapter is uncomplicated. It is that two-party job-oriented politics is characterized by political parties whose members are more concerned with jobs, contracts, and other sources of personal gain than with public policies. The job-oriented politician is concerned with issues only to the extent that they serve as a means of winning the elections that determine who holds office, which in turn determines who gains patronage. Another central characteristic of job-oriented political systems is a division of the electorate along lines unrelated to the problems that face the electorate.

A consequence of this style of politics is that elections are determined by a combination of traditional voting behavior together with responses to personalities and other nonissue variables. The voters, therefore, tend to be poorly informed concerning the relationship between their votes and their economic well-being. In fact, often there *is* no relationship. Thus, the citizen who is not concerned with jobs or contracts regards politics as a rather meaningless game.

Finally, the public policy product of job-oriented two-party politics is government which attempts—but not too hard—to please everyone. In particular, programs that reallocate goods and opportunities are minimized, for the low-income voter seldom casts his ballot in terms of economic self-interest—thereby enabling the politician to largely ignore his needs.

One-Party Politics

The stereotype of American politics is of two competitive political parties competing vigorously for the perquisites of power. At the national level this stereotype has approximated reality over most of the nation's history, with the candidates of the two major parties dividing the vote in fairly equal proportions.[1] However, before the Great Depression and World War II, one-party or weak two-party politics was the rule rather than the exception in most of the nation's states, counties, cities, and towns. Two-party politics superficially prevailed at the national level only because the numbers of one-party Republican and one-party Democratic localities were fairly equal. In the relatively few two-party states, such as Ohio, Indiana, Illinois, Missouri, Kentucky, and West Virginia, competition at the state level resulted from the rather equal divisions of the states into Republican and Democratic strongholds, partially as a result of the Civil War. In effect, these states resembled in microcosm the nation's political divisions.

The events of the Great Depression and World War II served to extend the two-party system to state and local levels in much of New England and the Middle West. The nationalizing influences of war and depression also had an impact on the politics of the South, the most isolated region of the nation. The Great Depression brought the federal government into the South in the role of protector and promoter of Southern economic interests through generous grant-in-aid programs, such as the Tennessee Valley Authority's efforts toward unified regional resource development. World War II further integrated the South into the nation through the movement of Southern whites and Negroes into the cities of the South and North and the movement of large numbers of Northerners into the South. Further, the war helped generate in the South a sense of national purpose that at least temporarily superseded regional grievances and aspirations. Over the period 1948-1964 the South gradually moved in the direction of a two-party system with respect to presidential politics.

However, one-party politics remained a characteristic feature of most of the South at the state and local levels and existed also in many localities in the North and West during the 1960's. As Table I showed, only nineteen states were strongly competitive (a score of 80 or more) between 1946 and 1958, and a majority of states remained one-party or weak two-party states in state elections. Consequently, one-party politics is a significant feature of the American political system.

The first step toward an understanding of American one-party politics is to distinguish it from Nazi party rule in Germany or Communist party rule in the Soviet Union. In most instances, single ruling parties at state and local levels are not monolithic centers of power that concentrate authority in one or a few hands. In a few instances, such as in plantation counties in the Deep South, where economic and social power is held by a very few leaders, the single political party becomes a vehicle through which large landowners exercise personal and arbitrary control over the lives and fortunes of the people in their domain. Before 1932, coal companies in Kentucky and West Virginia, steel companies in Pennsylvania, and railroads in many states used one-party systems at the local level as political means of enforcing their authority. However, most of the United States has had too pluralistic a power structure to permit the development of great concentrations of power in a single political party. There have been too many small farmers, too many small businessmen, and too many labor organizations to permit any individual or any small group to dominate a party.

Consequently, wherever a one-party system has existed in the United States, there has usually been continuing competition among various individuals and groups within the party, although some groups are frequently denied access to the party, such as Negroes in the Deep South. The groups fighting for control within a party are commonly referred to as "factions." In many respects, one-party factionalism is a primitive form of, and in some states closely resembles, two-party competition, while in other states factionalism is so chaotic that it might more accurately be described as no-party politics (or every man for himself).

In his classic study, *Southern Politics*,[2] V. O. Key classified the Southern one-party states in two broad categories of internal competition: one-party bifactional and one-party multifactional. In the following pages this classification will be used in describing the effects of one-party systems on public opinion and on government and the relationships of interest groups to one-party systems. First, however, it is necessary to inquire into some of the reasons for the existence of one-party political systems at the state and local levels.

CAUSES OF ONE-PARTY POLITICS

Table I provides a clue to the causes behind one-party politics. The table reveals that one-party and weak two-party states tend to be concentrated in the South, New England, and the Upper Midwest.

The Civil War marked the beginning of one-party politics in many states and sections. The Republican party was obviously identified with the North in the Civil War and with the attendant hardships suffered by many white Southerners, who generally agreed, therefore, that the Republican party was the enemy of the South. The only disagreement with this consensus was from Negroes and from pro-Union whites, who were largely to be found among the non-slaveholding small farmers in the Appalachians. After the Civil War and until the removal of federal troops, a two-party system existed in the South, with the Republican vote cast largely by Negroes and marginal farmers. In the latter part of the nineteenth century Negroes were disenfranchised throughout the Deep South. Populists, such as "Pitchfork Ben" Tillman, were instrumental in depriving Negroes of the ballot because of fear that conservative plantation owners would control Negro votes. Thereafter, and until the post-World War II era, the South was an intensely one-party region.[3]

Similarly, in New England and the Upper Midwest, people were in virtually unanimous agreement that the war with the South was a just, noble, and necessary enterprise. After the Civil War, the residents of these areas tended to identify the

Democratic party with a lukewarm attitude toward the Union, at best, and, at worst, with treason.

Thus, one-party politics in both the South and the North developed largely out of the experiences of the Civil War. In states where there was substantial agreement on the Civil War, one party was dominant thereafter. Only in states where people disagreed sharply over the Civil War or where substantial immigration occurred after the war did a two-party system survive the war. In states such as Ohio, Indiana, Illinois, Missouri, Kentucky, and West Virginia, substantial elements of the population had their roots in the South and tended to sympathize with it during the war. The most extreme sympathizers were called "Copperheads." Not all Democrats were Copperheads, but almost all Copperheads were Democrats, because the Democratic party was the only viable political alternative to Lincoln and the Republican party. Consequently, in these states' wartime gubernatorial elections the Democratic party tended to be identified with a policy of appeasement toward the South, and this position attracted the votes of both Copperheads and many other citizens who were simply weary of the war.

After the Civil War the two-party division tended to harden along the lines developed during the war. In the sections of each state settled by Southerners, Democrats received most of the vote and maintained virtually one-party rule. On the other hand, in the sections settled by New Englanders, Republicans were dominant and received an overwhelming majority of the vote. The fairly equal division within certain states of people whose ancestors hailed from the South and from New England resulted in competitive two-party politics at the state level but in one-party politics at the local level.

In some localities, particularly in the North, immigrants who arrived in the United States after the Civil War and who consequently were not concerned with the issues of that war provided the foundations of a two-party system. The new arrivals were primarily from Ireland, Germany, Italy, Scandinavia, and Eastern Europe, rather than from England, as were most of the native Americans, and they were Catholic and Jewish rather than Protestant. Further, they were largely impoverished and lacking the kinds of occupational and educational skills possessed by the native Americans. Consequently, they found themselves alienated from the native Americans by differences in language and culture, in religion, in education, and in economic well-being. Since the Democratic party was a political counterpoint to the nativist-dominated Republican party, it attracted these working-class immigrants. This is one of the reasons for the continued existence of a two-party system in the United States—that is, the minority party tends to monopolize opposition and to provide a haven for all the outs. Because the South was relatively untouched by the flow of new populations, its Democratic one-party system was left largely undisturbed until after World War II.

MULTIFACTIONAL ONE-PARTY POLITICS

Multifactional one-party politics as practiced in the Southern United States is a primitive political form. In fact, "no-party" politics comes closer than one-party politics to describing political reality in multifactional states such as Alabama:

> Alabama has not been dominated over a long period by a single well-disciplined machine. Nor have there been in recent years well-organized competing machines. Political factions form and re-form. Leadership in statewide politics tends to be transient. New statewide leaders emerge, rise to power, and disappear as others take their place. Voters group themselves in one faction and then in another in the most confusing fashion. No orderly system prevails... for the recruitment, development, and advancement of political leaders. Rather the political process appears as a free-for-all, with every man looking out for himself.
>
> . . . .
>
> If the factions within the Democratic party of Alabama amounted to political parties, a candidate's strength would not be influenced appreciably by his place of residence. A well-knit group of voters and leaders scattered over the entire state would deliver about the same proportion of the vote to its candidate wherever he happened to live. A concern for issues (or at least for group success) would override local attachments. In a well-developed two-party situation, localism is minimized, if not erased, by a larger concern for party victory.[4]

Key's description of multifactional one-party politics in Alabama applies with some modification to the politics of many states in the Deep South and also to some Northern states. (See Table XI for a listing of Southern multifactional one-party states.) In addition, the politics of some weak two-party states contains elements of multifactionalism. Therefore, the effects of multi-factional politics on public opinion, interest groups, and government should be of general interest to students of politics.

RELATIONSHIP TO PUBLIC OPINION

Multifactional one-party politics has a deadening effect on public opinion. There is no institutionalized means by which individuals and groups can attempt to change their social and economic environment through political activity. Each candidate for elective office runs on his own. Therefore, a newly elected governor has no faction or group in the legislature or in the courthouses of the state to which he can turn for support.

Since there is no positive program presented to the voters in primary contests, most of the people active in politics on a day-to-day basis are exclusively job-oriented; there is seldom any other reason for political activity. In addition, there are no battles between the ins and the outs in multifactional states, because the coalitions are so amorphous that there is seldom a candidate in a primary who defends the outgoing administration. The incumbent governor is ordinarily barred from the primaries by constitutional provisions limiting the governor to one term or by custom (Governor Orville Faubus of Arkansas is an exception). The purpose of the one-term limitation is to assure frequent changes in the personnel of government, but the effect has been to guarantee the preservation of multifactional, issueless politics.

In the absence of any opportunity to continue an administration beyond one term and of any future political need to defend his stewardship, an incumbent governor experiences few if any pressures to assemble a program of accomplishment to which he can point with pride in an election campaign. In the absence of any record of accomplishment or of any defense of the incumbent administration in the primaries, there is no out faction that seeks election by exposing the inadequacies of the administration. Each election contest starts afresh with an entirely new set of characters, none of whom feels obliged to offer any policy blueprint to the voters.

In the absence of stable factions representing policy positions, the voter receives little or no political information or guidelines that enable him to associate his vote for a candidate with his economic self-interest except on a job basis. Under these circumstances the vote tends to be cast for candidates who have achieved local fame. This "friends and neighbors" vote provides no mandate for public policy; it represents only pride in a local boy's candidacy.

Frequently, in multifactional one-party states, as many as ten candidates vie for the nomination for governor. Each candidate is assured of the vote of his home town and surrounding villages and attempts, through promises of patronage, to form temporary alliances with local leaders in other sections of the state in order to secure the relatively small vote necessary for a plurality. In most Southern states a run-off primary is held between the two candidates with the most votes, if neither received an absolute majority of the vote; the victor is typically the candidate who is able to secure, again through promises of patronage, the support of several of the lesser candidates in the first primary. The winner of the primary is almost invariably elected governor (usually without opposition until the post-World War II period). After serving out his term, he quite frequently disappears from political sight, succeeded by another local boy who made good.

The voter watches the succession of governors with cynical amusement. If "his" local boy wins election, he hopes that a new highway will be built in the county and that the road near his home will finally be paved. In addition, he might be a successful candidate for a state job. Aside from these immediate personal gains, however, elections are meaningless exercises to him. The only issue discussed in such Southern states is that on which almost every white person is agreed—"Negroes should be kept in their place."

The white supremacy issue is one that Southern politicians like Governor George Wallace of Alabama have used since the Civil War as a technique for suppressing other issue cleavages. Historically, the results have been as unfortunate for the low-income white Southerner as for the Negro Southerner. The growth of Negro registration in the South in company with the rise of the Republican party should work substantial changes in the party system and, through the parties, on the economic rationality of Southern voters. The shape of the future may be discerned in developments in Louisiana, where large numbers of Negroes were registered to vote after 1948. In the 1955 Democratic primary, Earl Long won the nomination for governor by virtue of the vote he received from low-income whites and Negroes, who voted for Long because of his support of generous welfare and education programs. The same kind of coalition of low-income whites and Negroes may emerge in other Southern states as Negroes receive the ballot and as Southern racist politicians find that white supremacy is therefore no longer the key to electoral success.

RELATIONSHIP TO INTEREST GROUPS

In a political system such as Alabama's, those interests that become dominant fare well with respect to the amount they return to state government in the form of taxes and the benefits they receive in the form of governmental programs.

There are several reasons for the political success of dominant-interest groups in multifactional one-party states. First, due to the fragmented nature of politics, any opponent of the dominant groups who wishes to assemble a political machine that can upset the status quo faces a virtually impossible task. Occasionally, a rebel may win election—e.g., "Kissin'" Jim Folsom, a Populistic governor of Alabama who attacked big business, advocated higher taxes on the rich, and improved education and welfare programs for the less well-to-do. However, since the legislature was elected entirely independently of Folsom, he had no way of pushing his program through that body. Consequently, few of the reforms he advocated successfully completed the legislative obstacle course.

Another explanation for the congenial political atmosphere in multifactional one-party states for dominant-interest groups is the character of election contests. There is no party organization that fights for the election of a candidate and that attempts to persuade voters of the superior virtue of the candidate and his platform. Thus, every man is on his own and must provide enough currency to his name to attract votes. This means that he must have money for news media and for workers to broadcast his name throughout the state. And the only ready sources of such economic largesse are the dominant-interest groups, such as utilities, trucking lines, and banks.

By definition, there is no strong interest group at odds with other large interest groups in multifactional states; if there were, a bifactional form of one-party politics would develop. Therefore, in states with multifactional one-party systems, labor unions are usually weak, and politicians take pains to keep them impotent through right-to-work laws and various official and unofficial acts designed to discourage labor's organizational activities.

One of the dominant-interest groups in Southern multifactional politics is the white community. The success of the Alabama political system in discouraging Negro efforts to secure a redress of political grievances speaks for itself.

BIFACTIONAL ONE-PARTY POLITICS

In a one-party system the struggles for political power of necessity take place within the single party and typically between the groups that are dominant in the state, such as businessmen and farmers. In some states whose dominant groups are relatively clear-cut and stable, this intraparty struggle for power becomes quite similar to a two-party system and is called bifactional politics. In essence, like two-party politics, it is a struggle for political power between the ins and the outs. Frequently, the ins identify with the more well-to-do business and farm portions of the community, and, just as frequently, the outs tend to identify with the smaller farmers and businessmen — at least until they achieve the comfortable status of the in group.

Bifactional politics can take either a job-oriented or an issue-oriented form and most frequently includes elements of both. Interestingly, states with bifactional one-party politics in which there is also a weak opposition party tend to be the most job-oriented — e.g., Tennessee and North Carolina. Conversely, states with bifactional one-party politics in which there is almost no opposition from a second party tend to be more issue-oriented — e.g., Louisiana and Georgia (see Table IX). Virginia is a special case; there, two-party competition over the period 1946-1958 placed it in the category of a weak two-party state rather than a one-party state, but its very weak two-party system seems to have resulted in unifactional politics. The political machine of former Senator Harry F. Byrd virtually eliminated internal opposition because of the need for unity in general elections. Consequently, Virginians live under a political system that offers almost no viable alternatives, in terms of public policy, between ins and outs or even among "friends and neighbors."

RELATIONSHIP TO PUBLIC OPINION AND INTEREST GROUPS

In contrast to the voter in multifactional political systems, the voter in bifactional one-party states has, at a minimum, a choice between the organizational ins and the outs. At a maximum, he is asked to choose between candidates who identify with opposite ends of the economic spectrum — that is, the rich and the poor. The following discussion of the relationships between interest groups and political factions concerns the differing choices offered the electorate.

The relationship of interest groups to political factions in one-party bifactional political systems appears to be similar to that observed in two-party issue-oriented systems. For example, the Standard Oil Company entered the hurly-burly of Louisiana politics in direct opposition to Huey Long and his "soak the rich" program.[5] In North Dakota, South Dakota, and Minnesota, the Nonpartisan League (mainly a farm organization) provided factional opposition to Republican regulars from 1916 until the post-World War II period.

The key to the existence of bifactional one-party politics as opposed to multifactional politics would appear to be the ability of a group — such as the Nonpartisan League, a labor organization, or a small opposition party — to voice criticism that must be heeded by the dominant constellation of interests. In states such as Tennessee and North Carolina, the minority Republican party forces Democrats to develop a fairly cohesive in group which is regularly opposed in Democratic primaries by the out group. The political combat in these states is usually over jobs.

However, where almost no minority party exists and where a cleavage develops between interest groups, as in Louisiana, Georgia, and North Dakota, the voters will inevitably divide according to their positions on current issues. Everyone is agreed on political party identification and thus, presumably, on ancient issues, such as the Civil War. Therefore, the major interest groups are drawn directly into the political conflict as members of a faction rather than as outsiders attempting to influence political events.

The effect of factional competition in both job-oriented and issue-oriented bifactional states is that voters are provided with some useful guidelines for casting their ballots. The job-oriented factions in Tennessee and North Carolina defend or criticize the incumbent adminstration and offer the voters alternative policies and personalities. The issue-oriented factions of Louisiana offer voters slates of candidates who represent broad alternatives in public policy. The Long candidates in Louisiana, who advocate tax, welfare, and education programs specifically designed to reallocate goods and opportunities, receive their votes from low-income people. Their opponents, who advocate conservative government, are supported largely by the more well-to-do portion of the population. The result is an electorate that is able to relate the ballot to economic self-interest.

EFFECT ON GOVERNMENT PERFORMANCE

The final and most important question to be directed at a political system concerns the quantitative and qualitative nature of its "payoff" — what are its costs and rewards to the citizenry in terms of material and psychic well-being?

Table XI provides data on eleven Southern states that help answer the question. On the average, there are greater percentages of Negroes and whites registered to vote in the four bifactional one-party states than in the six multifactional one-party states or in the unifactional weak two-party state. The averages of the three categories of states do not differ appreciably with respect to per cent nonwhite or per cent urban. Virginia is the wealthiest of the eleven states, but the bifactional and multifactional states do not differ appreciably in wealth. However, the bifactional states, on

TABLE XI
Southern One-Party States and Virginia: Categories of Factional Politics and Political, Social, and Economic Data

States[a]	Two-party competition score, 1946–1958	Per cent of Negroes registered to vote, 1965[b]	Per cent of whites registered to vote, 1965[b]	Per cent nonwhite, 1960[c]	Per cent urban residents, 1960[c]	Per capita income, 1959[d]	Average education expenditure per pupil in ADA, 1959–1960[e]	Per capita state and local welfare expenditure (less federal), 1959–1960[f]
Bifactional one-party								
Georgia	01	44.0	74.5	28.6	55.3	$1553	$123.37	$6.54
Louisiana	01	32.0	80.4	32.1	63.3	1575	214.08	17.05
North Carolina	37	46.8	92.5	25.4	39.5	1485	140.82	4.17
Tennessee	34	69.4	72.9	16.5	52.3	1521	132.17	5.19
Average	18	48.5	80.1	25.6	52.6	$1533	$152.61	$8.24
Multifactional one-party								
Alabama	15	23.0	70.7	30.1	55.0	$1409	$117.09	$7.68
Arkansas	19	54.4	71.7	21.9	42.8	1322	111.71	5.34
Florida	24	63.7	84.0	17.9	74.0	1980	181.27	7.64
Mississippi	00	6.7	70.1	42.3	37.7	1162	79.69	3.98
South Carolina	00	38.8	78.5	34.9	41.2	1332	122.39	3.43
Texas	10	57.7	53.2	12.6	75.0	1908	208.88	5.78
Average	11	40.7	71.4	26.6	54.3	$1519	$136.84	$5.64
Unifactional weak two-party								
Virginia[g]	42	45.7	55.9	20.8	55.8	$1816	$145.56	$2.85

[a]Classifications from V. O. Key. Jr.. *Southern Politics.*
[b]*Congressional Quarterly Weekly Report.* March 26. 1965. p. 557
[c]U.S. Bureau of the **Census.** *County and City Data Book 1962.*
[d]U.S. Bureau of the Census. *Statistical Abstract of the United States, 1961.*
[e]Research Division. National Education Association. *Rankings of the States. 1960*

[f]U.S. Department of Commerce. Bureau of the Census. *Governmental Finances in 1959.*
[g]In Table II. states with a competition score of 0–39 were classified as one-party states and those with a score of 40–79 as weak two-party states. Virginia. with a competition score of 42. is therefore classified as a weak two-party state.

the average, largely due to Louisiana's substantial expenditures, spend appreciably more on education and welfare than either the multifactional one-party states or the unifactional weak two-party state. Virginia's small expenditure on these items is all the more remarkable in light of its greater wealth. Louisiana, which is the most issue-oriented of the bifactional states, spends by far the most on welfare and education.

The relatively low per capita incomes of all the one-party states ($2168 is the 1959 national per capita income) reflect one of the social costs inherent in a system of politics that excludes a portion of the population from participation in government. It should not be surprising that when the dominant groups in a society are able to systematically suppress the weaker elements of the population, many of the people are poorly fed, poorly housed, poorly clothed, and poorly educated, If Negroes represent 40 per cent of a state's population and if that 40 per cent is regularly deprived of educational and economic opportunities, then 40 per cent of the state's population will be economically and culturally deprived.

Differences in each classification in the percentages of the populations registered to vote reflect certain differences in the openness of the systems to participation in the political process. In bifactional states, the well-organized factions make wide appeals to the populace and draw large numbers of voters to the polls. In multifactional states, appeals to the voters are largely limited to "friends and neighbors," and many individuals and groups are left out of the political process. In Virginia, where the Byrd machine still holds sway, the Democratic primaries are virtually devoid of any form of competition, and the Democrats are almost certain to win general elections at the state level. Therefore, few efforts are made to draw large numbers of voters into the political process.

The governmental payoff is that elected officials in bifactional one-party states frequently feel it necessary to sponsor education and welfare programs designed to reallocate goods and opportunities. In multifactional one-party states and in the unifactional weak two-party state, victorious politicians feel few if any such pressures to respond to the appeals of less privileged citizens.

The above analysis of one-party state politics concludes the investigation of state political party forms. In the following chapters we turn to the national two-party political system and the future of both state and national party politics.

National
Two-Party Politics

It has become a commonplace that the national Democratic and Republican parties are extremely weak confederations of fifty state parties united only by their common desire to capture the presidency. In the not-so-distant past there was much truth to this observation, and the parties in the 1960's still remained something less than unitary, well-disciplined organizations manned by like-minded militants at national, state, and local levels. However, the most striking trend in American politics after World War II has been the continuing deterioration in the strength of state and local parties, a deterioration that originated in the reform movements of the early twentieth century and that was accompanied by the growing power of national political institutions. The thesis of this chapter is that American national political institutions are relatively strong and influential and that their strength is increasing almost geometrically as state job-oriented parties wither away.

Historically, the basic cause of weakness in the national parties was the federal form of government, which provided each state with duties and bases of authority independent of the national government and national parties. The gradual disappearance of state political jobs due to civil service laws and nonpartisan forms of local government tended to break down the institutional barriers to the development of strong national parties.

Following World War II, the departure of job-oriented politicians from state and local organizations left vacuums that often were filled by issue-oriented individuals and groups. Labor unions, labor leaders, liberals, women with time on their hands and a concern for issues became active in state Democratic parties, and two kinds of issue-oriented Republicans emerged. The first is typified by George Romney of Michigan, Nelson Rockefeller of New York, and William Scranton of Pennsylvania, who believed that mid-twentieth-century America was a good place to live and who emphasized the desirability of an environment that encouraged excellence (*cf.* the Horatio Alger myth) rather than egalitarianism. The second type of issue-oriented Republican was unhappy with mid-twentieth-century America and harkened back to the nineteenth century as the nation's Golden Age. In 1961 Republicans of this second type organized a national secretariat outside the party which worked at infiltrating and seizing control of moribund Republican organizations at precinct, city, county, and state levels. The success of their efforts was made apparent by the nomination of Senator Barry Goldwater at the 1964 Republican National Convention.

That convention was not a traditional gathering of state Republican party representatives intent upon nominating the candidate most likely to win the election in order to administer the status quo more sensibly and enhance the federal job-securing prospects of the state party and the election prospects of the state ticket. On the contrary, the convention was dominated by a conclave of conservative militants who did not consider themselves representatives of a state party and who were not concerned with jobs. Helping the state ticket in the 1964 general elections was only a minor element in their calculations. Rather, the conservative Republican delegates were assembled to nominate a man who represented their policy views and who would capture a nationwide audience for those views. It is indeed paradoxical that a convention so preoccupied with states' rights embodied the most advanced development of strong national political parties. The 1964 Republican National Convention, which deplored the expansion of the powers of the national government, was not only a herald but also a precipitant of the concomitant decline of state parties and enhancement of national power and authority.

In the Democratic party, too, the issue-oriented state parties sent to the national conventions of 1952, 1956, 1960, and 1964 militant liberals and representatives of interest groups whose attention was fixed almost exclusively on national problems and policies rather than on state elections and jobs. Their votes helped nominate Adlai Stevenson in 1952 and 1956 and John F. Kennedy in 1960; and their influence was consistently directed toward strengthening the national Democratic party.

NATIONAL PARTY ORGANIZATIONS

Earlier chapters have shown that the performance of state government is related to the nature and organization of party competition. Our attention now turns to the organizational and informal means by which the several kinds of state parties assemble themselves into two competitive national parties. In so doing, we will observe the effects of state organizations on the nature of the national parties.

The primary organizational forms that comprise the national parties are the national conventions, the national committees, the national chairmen, the parties in Congress (caucus, floor leaders, steering or policy committees, and campaign finance committees), the President and his political apparatus (cabinet, executive office, formal and informal advisers), and the titular leader of the opposition party (the presidential candidate defeated in the preceding election).

Obvious features of the national party organization are the diffusion of power and authority and the absence of effective sanctions over state and local parties—witness the problem of "disloyal" Democrats in Southern states. Critics who fix their attention on these attributes of the American national parties frequently compare them unfavorably with the British parties and the parliamentary system of government within which they function, maintaining that the more nationalized and better disciplined British parties provide true party government and party responsibility. Specifically, they point to the fact that the prime minister and the minority party leader can ordinarily rely upon the support of their party's members in Parliament because of the sanctions at their command (e.g., the power to deny dissidents a place on the party's ticket at the next election, to eject them from the party, to grant or refuse them cabinet appointments, and to virtually ostracize them from all political association and activity). By virtue of such powers, the Labour party in 1965 was able to retain control of the British government with only a two-vote majority, because virtually every Labour party member could be counted upon to follow the lead of Prime Minister

Harold Wilson. When a British citizen casts his ballot for a Labour or a Conservative candidate, he knows that his choice, if victorious, will unswervingly support his party's platform. Some critics of the American party system recommend changes that would create similar party discipline and loyalty in the Senate and the House. The implicit—or, occasionally, explicit—assumption behind the recommendation is that a more unitary rather than federal form of government and more concentrated rather than separated powers would be beneficial to the citizenry of the United States. Surprisingly, the political and governmental reality that is emerging from the American federal system, despite its division of powers, is not so distant from the British model as its critics sometimes claim.

The Democratic and Republican national conventions and national committees are the creatures of the state parties, not their masters. National committee members from each state are selected by an instrument of the state party (usually the delegates to the national convention or the state central committee), and delegates from each state to the national convention are selected by a party convention in most states or by a popular presidential primary election. In practice, this means that if the leaders and personnel of the state parties have little in common except a desire for jobs, the national conventions and committees are little more than confederations of independent barons; but if the state political leaders and personnel share a common frame of reference concerning the objectives of the party, then the national conventions and committees can be cohesive and effective organizational expressions of national political unity.

CAUSES OF PARTY NATIONALIZATION

Since World War II both the Democratic and Republican national conventions and national committees have derived from a mixture of job-oriented and issue-oriented state parties. However, the trend has been toward a larger representation of issue-oriented segments, as evidenced by the increasing number of delegates in both parties to whom an issue such as civil rights or "voluntary social security" is more important than party victory.

One reason for the trend has been cited—the reduction of state patronage because of civil service laws. Other causative factors include the nationalization of central domestic problems, such as unemployment and prosperity, during the New Deal; the nationalizing effect of mass media, such as newspapers, periodicals, radio, and television; mass transportation, which facilitated the movement of a vast proportion of the population across state lines each year; and the enormously increased importance of foreign and military affairs, especially wars and cold wars. By the 1960's relatively few Americans thought of themselves primarily as citizens of Massachusetts or Illinois or any other state. Most thought of themselves, first, as citizens of the United States. In sum, there is a sequential relationship from (1) the Great Depression and the New Deal, mass media, mass transportation, wars and cold wars, to (2) the seizure of state parties by issue-oriented groups, to (3) the strengthening and nationalizing of the Democratic and Republican parties through the selection of delegates and committee members with a national issue orientation rather than a state job orientation, and finally to (4) the nomination and election of congressmen and senators who are more responsive to national political party leadership.

THE GREAT DEPRESSION AND THE NEW DEAL

Prior to the Great Depression and the New Deal, there were tentative moves in the direction of collective solutions to individual problems at both the federal and state levels. In 1914 the federal government smiled benignly though ineffectually on labor unions. In Wisconsin, Minnesota, and North Dakota attempts were made to solve labor, farm, and business problems through measures ranging from unemployment insurance through state ownership and operation of granaries. The Great Depression and the New Deal marked a turning point; this was the period of most rapid change away from the frontier-inspired rejection of collective approaches. Since the individual laborer could no longer find his employer in order to negotiate satisfactory wage contracts, he had to help finance a representative's trip to the corporate offices to bargain collectively for all the workers in the plant. Similarly, the farmer who sold in an individualistic, uncontrolled market, where prices were determined by supply and demand, found himself trapped by the necessity to purchase his farm equipment and other material in a controlled market. If the demand for farm equipment declined, manufacturers simply closed their plants, thereby reducing the supply of equipment and keeping the price high. The farmer, however, could not stop producing wheat or corn or tobacco when demand declined; on the contrary, he usually produced more of his product in an effort to make up in quantity the profits he lost through lower prices, with the result that prices dropped out of sight. The farmer then found it necessary to request that the government effect a collective solution to the problem by providing a "parity" price for farm goods accompanied by controls on production. Thus through collective action the farmer secured the same advantages in terms of production and price controls as did the manufacturers of steel or automobiles or farm equipment. However, prior to the Great Depression the individual solution of individual problems made practical sense in most of America's small towns and on the farms. The person who labored long and hard generally prospered, according to widely accepted myth (a myth that had some factual substance, however), while the loafer and the ne'er-do-well suffered economic privation. If a respected citizen suffered illness or death, his friends and neighbors provided the family with needed help. Each man and his family reaped the appropriate harvest from the seeds sown. God was in His heaven and all was right with the world.

When the depression struck,[1] farmers in Vermont received so little for their milk from the milk distributors that they were unable to pay their bills. In the granite quarries, machine shops, and textile mills of small-town Vermont, the industrious and provident person suffered equally with the idle and profligate. The harder they toiled, the more money they lost.

The immediate reaction to the economic tragedy was a form of collective action that was nevertheless in keeping with the American individualist tradition. The Vermont farmers attempted to help themselves by forming cooperatives, which sought to negotiate contracts with the milk companies and to regulate the production of milk. However, the milk companies consistently succeeded in breaking the cooperatives by purchasing only from independent farmers at a relatively generous price. As soon as the cooperatives disbanded to share in the proceeds, the price of milk plummeted back to one or two cents a quart. The farmers were then forced to seek governmental aid.

Homeowners, workingmen, bankers, and large and small businessmen all suffered similar experiences. Each turned to government for national and collective solutions to their problems. Through government-enforced negotiation and authorization of marketing agreements between producers and distributors, the Boston milk companies were forced to pay a "fair" price for milk, and, in turn, they endorsed "forced" limitations on the marketing of milk by individual farmers. Workingmen benefited by the National Labor Relations Act (1935), which compelled employers to engage in collective bargaining with union representatives. Bankers received a "holiday" in 1933, which temporarily closed the doors of banks to worried depositors; various other forms of government aid and support, including federal insurance of savings accounts, relieved bankers of pressures to return savings. Businessmen voluntarily moved toward collective efforts to

control production and prices through the National Industrial
Recovery Act (1933). As welfare funds were exhausted, the previously independent states, cities, and towns gratefully accepted
Works Progress Administration, Public Works Administration,
and Civilian Conservation Corps programs for unemployed
workers. Other collective efforts to solve individual problems
included social security, public assistance, and unemployment
compensation.

In short, out of the experience of prolonged depression and
New Deal reforms, attitudes toward collective efforts to solve
problems gradually changed. The collective solutions more and
more involved the federal government because city and state
efforts proved inadequate. The era of the frontier had passed,
having lingered long after the frontier was gone. Thousands of
youths who had suffered hardship and received succor from the
Civilian Conservation Corps, the National Youth Administration,
and other New Deal agencies emerged from the era with percep-
tions of their environment radically different from those previously held by residents of small towns and rural America. Many
had a crusading desire to remake the economic and social world
according to the more advanced objectives of the New Deal—
economic planning and cradle-to-grave security for the individual.
Millions who were not crusaders nevertheless came to accept the
necessity of governmental action, having been persuaded during
the Great Depression that many economic problems are national
problems. Many more millions who reached maturity after the
Great Depression inherited these views and the goals of social
justice.

WORLD WAR II

World War II diverted Franklin Roosevelt and the New Deal
from the crusade for domestic social justice to, among other
things, a crusade against fascism in order to establish the "four
freedoms" throughout the world (freedom of speech, freedom
of worship, freedom from want, freedom from fear). The war
facilitated the nationalization of the two major political parties,
since both the parties and the American people were forced to
focus their attention on such national issues as isolationism and
intervention, price controls and the draft, wages and profits.

After World War II millions of intelligent and aggressive
young people, whose philosophies had been shaped by the experiences of national depression and international war, completed
their education under the national government's GI Bill, and
many settled in cities and states far removed from their birth-

places, where they were released from traditional local political ties and concerns. These developments furthered the spread of national-issue orientation. The experiences, education, and employment of these young people tended to push many into political activity in both parties. In thousands of localities they were dismayed by the provincialism, narrow horizons, incompetence, and job orientation of local political leaders and soon were plotting to seize the parties from the "dead hands" that controlled them.

This postwar generation provided the enthusiasm and hard work that enabled coalitions of liberals and labor people to seize the Democratic party in states such as Michigan,. Minnesota, and Wisconsin, while similar groupings of middle management and professional personnel obtained working control of the Republican party in these and other states. Because the new Republicans and Democrats tended to be nationally oriented, their efforts were directed at strengthening the national parties through political activity at state and local levels. They worked to elect representatives and senators in Washington who would translate their policy preferences into law and governmental action.

PARTY LEADERS AND INTEREST GROUPS

The seizure in May 1964 of the Democratic party of Cincinnati, Ohio, by such a group of nationally oriented liberal Democrats is one of the more recent manifestations of the nationalization of American politics. Robert Kaplan, who was born in New York City and educated at Harvard University, had established a law practice in Cincinnati after World War II, following a brief period of employment with the United Nations. Kaplan was a child of depression and war, devoted to the social and economic objectives of the New Deal. In Cincinnati he combined a successful law practice with activity in liberal and reform organizations, ranging from committees to support the United Nations to the "good government" Charterites. Kaplan and others like him—fellow attorneys, university professors, some labor leaders, and other liberal citizens—found the conservative political climate in Cincinnati stifling, and they met frequently in organizations devoted to liberal causes. Their conversations inevitably turned to the need for a Democratic party in Cincinnati that would genuinely challenge the Republicans and provide the voters with meaningful policy alternatives.

Finally, in 1963, Kaplan and scores of other like-minded liberals decided to make an attempt to seize control of the city's Democratic party. They found approximately eight hundred liberals who were willing to run for election as precinct delegates to the Democratic county committee, obtained the required number of signatures for each candidate, and, in May of 1964, provided Democratic voters with a choice between the old job-oriented leadership and the newer issue-oriented leadership. The issue-oriented liberals emerged from the primary with a seven-vote plurality and were therefore able to replace the incumbent Democratic county chairman (an ex-professional football player) with one of their men (a liberal attorney). Subsequently, the new issue-oriented Democratic leadership secured the nomination of another liberal attorney, John J. Gilligan, to run for election to the seat of Robert Taft, Jr., in the U.S. House of Representatives. Gilligan defeated his Republican opponent in the 1964 election and provided President Johnson with unswerving support, as a congressman, for his legislative program.

The total impact of issue-oriented people upon the Democratic and Republican parties is difficult to measure quantitatively. However, the broad scope of that impact is a bit clearer in the Democratic than in the Republican party, both because the Democratic party has ruled nationally over most of the period from 1932 to 1966 and because the people most directly affected by war and depression have tended to turn to the Democratic party. The following discussion deals largely with the Democratic party, therefore, but it should be kept in mind that the thousands of people who draw their political inspiration from the Rockefellers, Romneys, Scrantons, and Hatfields are taking part in a similar developmental process within the Republican party.

Within the Democratic party, scores of issue-oriented liberals have represented their states on the platform committee of the national conventions, where they have fought for planks endorsing Medicare, expanded social security programs, and federal action to protect and expand the civil rights and liberties of minority groups. They have also provided a solid bloc of support for liberal Democratic candidates as nominees for President and Vice-President. Perhaps most importantly, they have transmitted the ideas, policy innovations, and ideological underpinning for Northern Democrats in both the party conventions and Congress. This ideological foundation has provided the Democratic party with an institutionalized commitment to liberal objectives and has thereby affected the behavior of Northern job-oriented Democrats as well as issue-oriented Democrats.

CONGRESS

In Congress the issue-oriented Democrats helped organize liberal study groups that pushed the more conservative leadership toward action on liberal-supported programs. In fact, the liberals have succeeded in defining the central spirit of the Democratic party. They are its motivating and driving force and have helped make the presidential Democratic party a truly national party for the first time since the Civil War. The national Democratic party today means very nearly the same thing in Mississippi and Vermont as in New York and Michigan and California. More and more, it represents a package of policy ideas to which all voters react, either negatively or positively. No longer is it the white man's party in the South and the Irish Catholic's party in New England; it has instead a national identity that transcends geographical and sociological boundaries.

The development of strong national political parties has had a profound impact upon the voting behavior of United States senators and representatives and on the public policy products emanating therefrom. James Burns saw the Republicans and Democrats in Congress as members of parties distinct from and hostile to the national presidential parties in his excellent book *The Deadlock of Democracy*.[2] Burns' thesis was historically accurate, but at the very time that he was decrying the Democratic congressional party's effect on President Kennedy's legislative program, that portion of the party was in the process of dissolution. The success of President Johnson in obtaining the enactment of a mass of national legislation during his first year in office signified the continuing decay of the congressional parties.

Perhaps the best approach to an understanding of the changes that have taken place in the political orientation of congressmen is to compare the Democratic vote for Franklin Roosevelt's legislative program in the one-sidedly Democratic 75th Congress (1937-1938) with the vote for Kennedy's New Frontier and Johnson's Great Society in the 88th Congress (1963-1964).

In his 1936 landslide victory over Republican Alfred M. Landon, F.D.R. carried into office with him a Senate consisting of 75 Democrats and only 17 Republicans (4 miscellaneous) and a House with 337 Democrats and 89 Republicans (13 miscellaneous). In spite of these Democratic majorities, however, Roosevelt enjoyed little success in obtaining the enactment of his legislative program. Figure 3 identifies the source of his legislative problems in the Senate by showing the Democratic vote on one important bill in his legislative program. The anti-Roosevelt votes came from non-Southern solons with a great deal of seniority. Almost 60 per cent of the non-Southern Democrats first elected in 1930 or before voted against Roosevelt's bill, as did more than 50 per cent of those elected in 1932. Similarly, Southern Democratic senators with the most seniority were more likely than their

Figure 3

Effect of Seniority on Senate Voting

Per cent of Democrats supporting a motion to recommit
Franklin Roosevelt's Judiciary Reorganization Bill
to the Judiciary Committee, July 1937

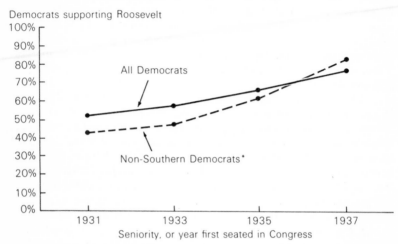

SOURCE: David R. Mayhew, "The Defeat of Roosevelt's Administrative Reorganization Bill," unpublished
seminar paper, Harvard University, 1960, p. 12.

junior colleagues to vote against Roosevelt, although Southern
senators in general (except those elected in 1936) were more
likely than non-Southern senators to support him.

The findings in Figure 3 generally validate Burns' thesis
concerning the nature of the political parties, for the Democratic
congressmen who blocked Roosevelt's legislative program in
1937-1938 identified with Congress as an institution and felt
little loyalty to or identification with the national presidential
party. Further, these congressmen came from states where the
Democratic organization was largely conservative and often
corrupt, controlled by job-oriented people during a period when
there were many jobs available for the party faithful. Therefore,
the local Democratic parties felt little need to subordinate their
preferences concerning candidates to F.D.R.'s policy demands.

Between the 75th Congress in 1937-1938 and the 88th
Congress in 1963-1964, important changes occurred in the nature
of the Democratic state parties outside the South and in the
political orientation of their candidates. In state after state and in
many cities, job-oriented Democrats lost their hold on the party
organizations to issue-oriented coalitions of liberals and union

leaders. In states such as Michigan, Minnesota, and Wisconsin, and in cities such as Cincinnati, Detroit, Milwaukee, and Los Angeles, issue-oriented Democrats elected issue-oriented congressmen who were presidential rather than congressional Democrats.

Figure 4 traces the breakdown of the non-Southern congressional Democratic party that culminated in 1963-1964. In the 88th Congress, the senators with considerable seniority were just as likely as those first seated in 1963 to support the Kennedy-Johnson legislative programs. In fact, more than 60 per cent of the non-Southern Democrats in every category of seniority cast their votes for administration programs; the Southern Democrats with greatest seniority cast most of the opposition Democratic votes.

Thus, outside the South, Democratic members of the 88th Congress supported the presidential programs without reference to seniority. By and large, they identified with the national presidential party rather than with Congress or the states. Senators such as Phil Hart of Michigan, Hubert Humphrey of Minnesota, and Joseph Clark of Pennsylvania were nominated and elected by Democratic state organizations because of their identification with the national presidential party, not because of services they might perform for conservative and corrupt job-oriented state parties.

Figure 4
Effect of Seniority on Senate Voting

Per cent of Democrats supporting the Kennedy-Johnson
administration in 212 roll calls during 1963–1964

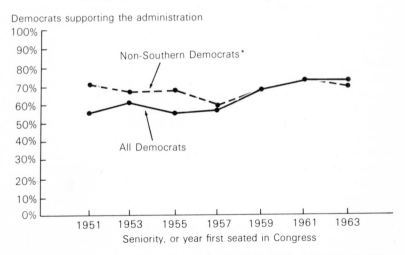

SOURCE: *Congressional Quarterly Weekly Report,* March 13, 1964, p. 526, and October 30, 1964, p. 2595.

In the South, the relationship of support for presidential policies and senatorial seniority assumes significance in the light of the development of two-party competition in many Southern states. According to an article by Raymond Wolfinger and Joan Heifetz,[3] only 166 of the 294 Democratic seats in the South could be considered "safe" after the 1964 election. Therefore, the national presidential Democratic party could count on increased support from Southern congressmen also.

As the Democratic party becomes more cohesive and as Northern Democratic dominance increases, there is a tendency to read rebellious Southerners out of the party. In 1964 Senator Strom Thurmond of South Carolina voluntarily shifted his allegiance from the Democratic to the Republican party, recognizing that the liberal national character of the Democratic party made it virtually impossible for him to achieve his conservative ends within the party. On January 2, 1965, the Democratic caucus in the House of Representatives stripped seniority rights within the party from Representatives John Bell Williams of Mississippi and Albert Watson of South Carolina, who had supported Barry Goldwater in the 1964 presidential election. The caucus action robbed the two rebel Democrats of influential committee assignments and interrupted their progress through tenure toward posts as committee chairmen. Not surprisingly, it was a liberal Democrat, Representative John A. Blatnik of Minnesota, who introduced the motion. There is evidence of centralizing tendencies in all of the Democratic party's national organs. Northern issue-oriented members of the party dominate the convention scene and show an increasing willingness to read nonconformist elements out of the party by denying them representation in conventions.[4] In Congress, liberal Democrats have succeeded in punishing the most extreme conservative Southern dissidents for failure to support the national presidential candidate, and they can be expected to demand even greater conformity to the party's liberal platform as they move into more and more positions of power through increased seniority.[5] In the Democratic National Committee, the Michigan, Minnesota, and Wisconsin issue-oriented party organizations are regarded as models to emulate at both the national and state levels. Neil Staebler, the former Michigan State Democratic Chairman, is frequently called upon to provide ideas and direction for other state Democratic party organizations. After 1952, when the Democrats were out of power, the national committee appointed a study group of distinguished liberal Democrats to help provide party guidance independent of congressional leadership. The study group was additional evidence of a movement in the Democratic party toward seeking national answers to problems and of an attempt to organize the party so as to direct the eyes of the nation toward the national policy positions of a unified party.

As a result of depression and war, the Republican party, too, became a more issue-oriented and nationally oriented party. Actually, the Republican party had never been as job-oriented as the Democratic party, due in part to the fact that the majority of its members were white Anglo-Saxon Protestants who had less interest in patronage than did the disinherited immigrants in the Democratic party. In addition, the Republicans had a clearer idea of the "good society," which to them meant fairly equal opportunities for all to compete for the "good things of life" and minimum restraints on the individual as he did so. This was a comfortable philosophy for those Americans who had first settled the country and who therefore enjoyed a substantial lead in the pursuit of property and position.

After 1945 substantial numbers of liberal, issue-oriented Republicans were willing to recognize the need for governmental programs to redistribute goods and opportunities. However, they insisted that their goal was not an egalitarian society but an environment that would insure the realization of the basic Republican goal—optimum individual development with a minimum of restraints. Other issue-oriented Republicans who were not as directly affected by depression and war sought to return the national party to its pre-1936 moorings. In 1963 and 1964 the conservative Republicans succeeded in obtaining control of state organizations, partially due to the fact that the Republican party in many of these states was an empty shell. After the overwhelming defeat of Goldwater in 1964, issue-oriented liberal and moderate Republicans contended with conservatives for control of the party. In 1966 the outcome of the struggle between these factions remained in doubt.

THE PRESIDENT

In the last analysis, though, the most important single formative influence on the party system has been the President. In his 1965 State of the Union message to Congress, Johnson spoke as the leader of a national Democratic party dedicated to the solution of the individual's problems on the farms and in the cities, towns, and suburbs. His message contained a "national agenda," which included "a program in education to ensure every American child the fullest development of his mind and skills...a massive attack on crippling and killing diseases...a national effort to make the American city a better and more stimulating place to live."

But this was only the preamble. President Johnson also proposed programs to develop underprivileged areas, control crime and delinquency, eliminate every obstacle to the right to vote, develop high-speed rail transportation between cities, provide hospital care for the aged, double the war against poverty, enforce the civil rights law, make a massive effort to beautify the countryside, prevent pollution of air and water, establish a national foundation for the arts, and encourage basic science. The President felt confident of the support and help of a reasonably united national Democratic party in Congress, in the national committee, and at the state and city levels in securing the translation of his policy objectives into law. His confidence was based not upon faith but upon the votes he could count on in both houses of Congress — votes that would support his program because of party agreement on means and ends.

Thus, the Democratic party has become an effective national political instrument. The difference between Johnson's one-sided Democratic majorities in Congress in 1965 and Franklin Roosevelt's even larger majorities in 1937 is a strong testimonial to the nationalization of the American political parties. Roosevelt was unable to depend upon the support of his Democratic congressmen, many of whom were the nominees of conservative and job-oriented state party machines, whereas the non-Southern Democrats in Congress in 1965 were primarily liberals whose candidacies had been promoted by transformed state and local political machines. Johnson could face the 89th Congress with little or no fear of a repetition of Congress' revolt against Roosevelt and the New Deal, partially because his election helped pull so many into office but predominantly because they were liberals. In fact, the more likely prospect in 1965 was that the liberal Democratic majorities would press Johnson for more rather than less liberal and reform legislation.

Thus, it could no longer be said that the national political parties were weak and impotent, although the factional disputes among issue-oriented Republicans left the ultimate fate of that party temporarily undecided. True, the United States was still a federal union of states, and, true, the one hundred Democratic and Republican state parties were relatively independent of the national parties in an organizational sense. There was no way in which the national parties could control the actions of the state or city parties, which, formally, could still nominate any candidate and assume any policy position they wished.

The Republican and Democratic national chairmen and national committees remain groups with few sanctions to coerce the state parties. They can appoint study committees, adopt lofty statements of party principle, plead for party unity, and print and distribute party propaganda; but they cannot issue orders to any party functionary outside the national committee, and they have precious few sticks with which to prod party leaders. Their only important formal functions are to issue the quadrennial call for a national convention, select a time and place for the convention, and appoint its temporary officers.

Congress is still, as it always has been, the single locale at which the two parties organize on a national level in order to work out solutions to national problems. In large part, congressmen still represent states or parts of states and are thus the spokesmen of rather localized interests. Consequently, despite their progress toward national organization, the two parties in Congress are by no means entirely coherent executors of party principle.

The President, although the head of his party, lacks many of the tools necessary to ensure conformity to the party program in Congress or at state and local levels. The separation of powers between the executive and legislative branches combined with the dwindling patronage at his command makes it difficult to secure compliance from congressmen who are disinclined to support party goals. Similarly, federalism constitutes a political wall around each state which protects local party machines from direct control by the President.

But when all this is said, it remains true today that the two political parties are relatively effective and homogeneous national units, striving in a fairly concerted way to achieve the party's goals through national action, albeit divided by moderate-conservative factionalism within the Republican party and Northern-Southern factionalism in the Democratic party.

SUMMARY

We have already mentioned many of the reasons for the development of surprisingly cohesive national parties, but it would be useful to summarize them here. The fundamental cause of developing nationalism in the parties is the increasing homogeneity of the American people, produced by the settlement of the continent and the strict limitations placed on immigration from countries outside Western Europe in the 1920's, combined with the spread of the mass media. Americans from coast to coast generally wear the same kinds of clothes, root for the same football and baseball teams, mourn the loss of a President, and yearn for the same automobiles.

The American of the 1960's thinks of the United States in singular rather than plural terms. Instead of a concern for states' rights and separation of powers, many Americans have exaggerated notions of the power of the central government and the President. It came as a shock to most Americans that federal police did not take charge in Dallas after President Kennedy's assassination; following that tragic event, assassination of the President was made a federal offense. In short, we tend to look more and more to our national government and national leaders for guidance and aid, both because we face more problems that are obviously national (e.g., war, defense, and foreign policy) and because we tend to view as national certain problems that earlier generations regarded as local (e.g., depression and poverty).

Depression and war also accelerated nationalization. The shared suffering and the shared relief of victory in 1945 brought unity of mind and spirit. In particular, those who shared the experiences of depression and war emerged from them with a spirit that President Johnson movingly recaptured in his 1965 State of the Union message, when he said, "No longer can anyone wonder whether we are in the grip of historical decay. We know that history is ours to make. And if there is great danger, there is now also the excitement of great expectations."

The American of the 1930's and 1940's had been freed from the hobbles of laissez-faire economics, which held that a competitive economic system would work best if government confined itself to narrowly defined police activities. He had found, however, that the citizen together with government could harness rivers, provide economic security, develop bombs capable of protecting or destroying it all—and yet maintain a dynamic, privately owned, competitive economy. Thus, there was born a new tendency to turn to the national government for the solution of problems that had seemed insoluble—floods and flood control, soil erosion and soil conservation and reforestation, drought and irrigation, depression and pump priming, slums and public housing and urban redevelopment, strikes and labor relations, poverty and social security. Science and technology and the political processes rendered national solutions feasible.

After World War II the political parties at the state level were, in many instances, empty shells, a condition caused by civil service laws and the comparative unattractiveness of patronage jobs in a period of prosperity. As the job-oriented political parties decayed, new issue-oriented parties with a national inclination emerged. In Michigan, the United Auto Workers in company with liberals from the professions, business, and elsewhere took over the Democratic party, and individuals from middle management and the professions obtained control of the Republican party. In Minnesota, labor union leaders, liberals in the universities, women,

and former members of the Farmer Labor party captured the
Democratic party, and a coalition of women and politically minded
businessmen and professional people dominated Republican
politics.

In 1964 the trends set in motion by the 1929 stock market
crash culminated in one of the most issue-oriented elections in
American history. The predictable success of the presidential
candidate who advocated specific national means of solving
national problems produced an administration pledged to preside
over final national unification. As President Johnson expressed
it in his 1965 State of the Union message:

> We are entering the third century of the pursuit of
> American union.
>
> Two hundred years ago, in 1765, nine assembled
> colonies first joined together to demand freedom from
> arbitrary power.
>
> For the first century we struggled to hold together the
> first continental union of democracy in the history of man.
> One hundred years ago, in 1865, following a terrible test
> of blood and fire, the compact of union was finally sealed.
>
> For a second century we labored to establish a unity
> of purpose and interest among the many groups which
> make up the American community.
>
> That struggle has often brought pain and violence. It
> is not yet over. But we have achieved a unity of interest
> among our people unmatched in the history of freedom.
>
> And now in 1965 we begin a new quest for union. We
> seek the unity of man with the world that he has built —
> with the knowledge that can save or destroy him — with the
> cities which can stimulate or stifle him — with the wealth
> and machines which can enrich or menace his spirit.[6]

The American Political Future

The social scientist or casual visitor or lonely aged person cannot help but note the need for a community of feeling and action in the United States. Until very recently most people felt themselves a secure and comfortable part of a family, a profession, or a craft. Psychological or monetary support was usually available through family or friends. The individual standing naked and alone, without family or friends, is a unique mid-twentieth-century development. Until the last two or three decades most urbanites had a farm or a homeland to return to (or at least to dream of) in the event of failure. The typical 1960 American has no support other than his wife and his insurance agent.

The crippling effect on the nation of such jungle-like isolation can never be quantified, although some notion of its magnitude may be gained by comparing the achievements of American Jews, who do live in a community where the individual receives support, with the American Negro, who in most cases must fight life's battles unaided by the support of any community.

ISOLATION VS. COMMUNITY

Most American Jews are first-, second-, or third-generation immigrants. Judging by the experiences of other immigrant groups in our society, first- and second-generation Jews should still be painfully struggling at the bottom of the socioeconomic ladder. Studies show, however, that the Jewish people, far from doing the dirty work of the society, are leading the American "rat race" in many lines of endeavor.[1] Fewer Jews than other groups are engaged in manual labor, and proportionately more are in the professions. Jews even outperform, in terms of income and occupation, such white Anglo-Saxon Protestant groups as Episcopalians and Congregationalists, who traditionally have been considered our country's most successful citizens. What, then, distinguishes Jews from other groups?

One common answer is that Jews are unusually competitive as a result of the discrimination and prejudice they have so often encountered. Being victimized by discrimination hardly seems an adequate explanation, however, for if this were the case, Negroes would outperform all other groups in society. Other hypotheses explaining Jewish success in the United States are that they have great respect for education and that their "middle-class" training in Europe equipped them for the social and economic struggle in the United States. However, granting that each of these factors and others have contributed to Jewish upward mobility, the variable most responsible for giving them effect has been the Jewish feeling of community, which is reflected in their political as well as their social and economic behavior.

For example, members of the major ethnic and religious groups in the United States tend to be politically influenced as much or more by economic and social status as by ethnic or religious affiliations. Among Baptists, Episcopalians, Congregationalists, Catholics, and Methodists, upper-income members are more likely to vote Republican than low-income members. But Jews are the exception to the rule. Studies of Jewish voting behavior reveal that upper-income Jews are about as likely to vote Democratic as low-income Jews,[2] which indicates that their primary reference in terms of political behavior is their ethnoreligious group rather than their class or occupational position. It is primarily due to this community of feeling among Jews that they have enjoyed such pronounced economic success in the United States. The American Jew has never been a lonely, isolated individual fighting by himself in the jungle of free enterprise. Jewish culture teaches that the rich are obligated to help the less fortunate and that the poor have a right to this help. From this community of feeling emerge social services that save Jews from economic catastrophe and enable many to attend college and, perhaps most importantly, a cohesive family that provides each child continuing guidance and support.

Compare to this secure community the plight of the isolated Negro, robbed of his culture and his leaders, fighting the battle for survival by himself. Until recently, Negroes had never formed a cohesive community, and the unhappy record of their failures teaches that the isolated individual almost always perishes. The Negro family is characterized by matriarchy and a degraded or absent father, and the Negro child is virtually on his own after birth. Only since the 1930's, when a community of attitude started developing among Negroes, have they begun to emerge from second-class citizenship.

The lesson for the nation contained in the comparison of Jewish and Negro experience should be apparent. If any group, whether it be a whole nation or an ethnic minority, feels bound together in the sense that the needs of each are a command on all, it is strengthened immeasurably. This seems so obvious that it should require no elaboration. However, the success of the American political right wing in obtaining a nationwide audience for its view that we should be a nation of wolves (and sheep) testifies to the need to drive home the unhappy implications of that creed.

THE 1964 PRESIDENTIAL CAMPAIGN

The nomination of Barry Goldwater by the Republican party in 1964 was one index of the success enjoyed by the advocates of atomization. Much of the press and the public, as well as political scientists, found the nomination difficult to understand. Everything seemed to militate against it. The eastern Republican establishment (Rockefeller, Scranton, and the financial community) almost unanimously opposed it and was joined in opposition by the majority of rank-and-file Republicans and Democrats alike, as indicated by polls and the results of primaries. Ultimately, virtually every leading newspaper expressed strong reservations about Goldwater's candidacy. The unimpressive 38.5 per cent of the total vote that Goldwater received (the smallest per cent of the total vote since Landon's 36.5 in 1936) only confirmed the worst fears and strongest arguments of the eastern Republican establishment.

Political scientists were particularly puzzled by Goldwater's nomination because they had assumed that electoral victory would be more important to the delegates than ideological purity. Therefore, they had expected the convention delegates to decide upon a middle-of-the-road candidate, as in 1952 when Eisenhower rather than Taft was nominated, because the delegates rightly expected Eisenhower to draw votes from the great cluster of independents and weak Democrats who straddle the fence dividing the right and left wings of the political spectrum. Nevertheless, Goldwater was nominated on the first ballot by more than a two-to-one majority. It was impossible to claim that he had "bought" the nomination or had secured it through wily intrigue. The enthusiasm of most delegates for Goldwater as a personality and as an advocate of right-wing policies was evident from the outset of the convention. By and large, the delegates did not appear to yield Goldwater their votes for self-seeking reasons or because of organizational pressures; rather, most lay their votes at his feet with as much rapture as Stevenson supporters had shown in 1952.

THE CONSERVATIVE MOVEMENT

The question is why the convention delegates were so out of tune with the Republican establishment, with the mass media, and with the public at large. The first clue to this modern political mystery is found in the number of zealots who were active in the Goldwater movement. Observers of the convention were startled by the intensity of emotion and the accompanying intolerance that characterized many of the delegates. The deafening boos that greeted Rockefeller's post-midnight attack on extremism and the approving cheers that followed Eisenhower's attack on television and newspaper commentators were symptomatic of the fact that the Republican delegates in 1964 were a breed apart.

The second piece to the Goldwater puzzle is the vote by states. Delegates from the sixteen states with Republican governors gave Goldwater less than half their votes (214 for Goldwater to 238 for his opponents), while delegates from the thirty-four states with Democratic governors preferred Goldwater by an almost four-to-one margin (699 to 187). The vote of the states with Republican governors would have been even more markedly anti-Goldwater if there had been a chance of defeating him, but, in resigned despair, many Republican leaders bent to the Goldwater wind.

These two observations are not unrelated. The incumbent Republican governors were, by definition, successful politicians. Although the more prominent among them — such as Scranton of Pennsylvania, Rockefeller of New York, Romney of Michigan, and Hatfield of Oregon — were as issue-oriented as their factional foes to the political right, the package of policy preferences with which they won election had been drawn from what they liked to call the "mainstream" of Republican and American thought and experience. At its center, this mainstream contained a profound satisfaction with and pride in American life in the 1960's. The substance of the satisfaction and pride was drawn from the nation's experience on the frontier, where men of humble origins seized the opportunities afforded by virgin land and built from the wilderness productive farms, enormous industrial complexes, great cities, and ultimately the most powerful nation in the world. The concrete policy preference that flowed from these accomplishments was a desire to maintain a frontier environment of equal opportunities by providing public education, welfare, and other programs to insure that each individual began at an approximately equal point. The Republican liberals specifically rejected the goal of an equalitarian society in favor of this equality of opportunity, where the only limit to an individual's horizons would be his own vision. The liberals were willing to use local, state, and national government resources, wherever necessary, to insure the maintenance of such frontier freedom of opportunity.

The airy formulas of the political extremists also grated harshly on the ears of job-oriented Republican leaders, who knew from experience and by intuition that those formulas did not provide a platform wide enough to accommodate a majority of the electorate. Successful state chairmen such as Ray Bliss of Ohio had learned that issues which divide the electorate along the lines marked out by conservatives are disastrous for the Republican party. For Bliss, the classic example of such an issue is "right-to-work," a proposed constitutional amendment that would have outlawed contract provisions between unions and management which required new employees of a company to join the union within a specified period of time. The proposal lost by an almost two-to-one margin in Ohio in a 1958 referendum—drawing affirmative votes only from small towns where unions were weak or nonexistent—and dragged to defeat the candidates for governor and United States senator, who had supported the proposal, and virtually the entire Republican state ticket. The experience proved conclusively that any candidate in Ohio who identifies himself with an anti-union position is committing electoral suicide. To Bliss and other professional Republican politicians, the 1964 Goldwater candidacy was a political equivalent of Ohio's referendum.

Perhaps more important in 1964 than the platform's limited appeal was the fact that hard-working practicing Republican politicians were made uncomfortable by the right-wing zealots. One Indiana Republican state leader told the writer in an interview that the Goldwater and Birch Society zealots in his state's party reminded him of the OAS (an organization, composed largely of French colons, that had violently opposed self-determination for Algeria). The Birchers were engaged in a holy war against the Democratic infidels.[3] The Republican professional was not a crusader but a workingman, trying as best he could to elect Republicans and to govern the state in such a way as to win re-election. He liked and respected individual Democratic leaders, who, after all, were fellow professionals doing a similar job with similar tools. The simple solutions to complex problems advanced by right-wing zealots offended the common sense based on experience of the Republican professionals who were currently finding those problems just as hard to solve as had their Democratic predecessors. Consequently, the delegates from states with Republican governors tended to vote for "moderate" Republican candidates, such as Scranton.

In both the states with issue-oriented and those with job-oriented Republican governors, the 1964 Republican party had state, county, and precinct leaders who were devoted to the governor or who made a living out of politics or both. Some of them had political jobs or political privileges, such as contracts, by virtue of actions of the incumbent Republican governor, or shared the policy preferences of issue-oriented liberal Republicans; in either case, they were alive to the governor's preferences, and they made every effort to nominate and elect state convention delegates and local-office candidates who were similarly responsive.

Republican party organizations in states with Democratic governors presented a markedly different scene in 1964. Democrats controlled the governor's office in thirty-four of the fifty states and in many of the thirty-four had been in control over much of the period since 1932. Therefore, the traditional job-oriented Republican leader had gradually disappeared—in fact, many Southern states had never had a viable Republican organization.

By 1964 great legions of issue-oriented, hardworking, sincere, and sometimes simple-minded conservatives had seized control of the Republican party in the thirty-four states with Democratic governors. Neither liberal nor moderate Republicans had effectively challenged them for a variety of reasons. First, no liberal or moderate Republican at the national level mobilized like-minded Republicans at the local level. Rockefeller's futile efforts in this direction were fatally handicapped by his personal problems. Other issue-oriented moderates were not particularly interested in obtaining the 1964 Republican nomination, feeling— quite justifiably—that such nomination would be a mixed blessing at best. President Kennedy's assassination and the subsequent wave of emotion that swept the American people seemed to assure Lyndon Johnson of an easy victory, regardless of the identity of his Republican opponent.

The motivating force behind the conservative movement in 1964 had much in common with the philosophy of the moderate and liberal Republicans. Both drew their inspiration from America's frontier experience, where hard work and enterprise were usually rewarded by wealth and privilege, while sloth and stupidity brought only meager harvests. Conservatives idealized this frontier past and advocated policies designed to return America to the golden heritage from which its strength, wealth, and greatness emerged. The specific policies demanded in order to secure this end were the elimination of governmental and union restraints on individual initiative (e.g., progressive income tax, minimum wage laws, maximum hour laws, collective bargaining by unions) and the elimination of governmental programs designed to reallocate goods and opportunities, which, according to conservatives, take from the industrious individual to provide for the slothful.

The basic problem in selling this program to the American people was the fact that the frontier and its limitless opportunities no longer exists in any concrete, physical sense. Interestingly, the conservative movement outside the South was strongest in the West, where the frontier experience was freshest in people's minds and where substantial amounts of land (albeit arid and unproductive land) remained unoccupied. In great metropolitan areas of the Midwest and the East and in the depressed coal areas of Kentucky, West Virginia, and Pennsylvania, the only visible frontier was grade school, high school, and college. Moreover, this frontier had to be manufactured by government in large part, and government had to help provide food and clothing as well as training if children were to reach even that frontier.

Thus, all Republicans started with the frontier experience as a model for the good life. However, the liberal or moderate contended that the maintenance of a frontier way of life required governmental programs designed to assure that everyone had an opportunity to find the frontier. The conservative, on the other hand, maintained that the frontier still existed for anyone with the energy and will to find it — perhaps not in the strict sense of free land, but at least in the 1890's sense of opportunities for business and other kinds of enterprise. In many states with Democratic governors these conservatives seized control of the Republican party in much the same way that the United Auto Workers and the ADA seized control of Michigan's Democratic party. They did it by working at the precinct level to elect local Republican leaders who were similarly oriented. In 1964 they succeeded in electing right-wing delegates to the state conventions, which in turn elected right-wing zealots to the national convention. The delegates were not moved by the traditionally effective appeal that an extreme conservative would lose. Of course they wanted desperately to win the election, but victory with a moderate would have been a defeat for their principles; and principles—spreading the conservative gospel—unquestionably were their main concern.

Barry Goldwater was the perfect political expression of the policy preferences of the issue-oriented conservatives attending the convention. He was not a typical job-oriented politician but, in a sense, a Republican Adlai Stevenson. Issue-oriented Democrats had applauded Stevenson because, when he spoke in oil-rich Louisiana as well as in New York, he consistently and straight-forwardly advocated that the federal government retain tidelands oil. In like manner, conservative Republicans found relief from the smoke-choked political atmosphere of the past in Goldwater's style of meeting opponents head-on, regardless of the electoral consequences. They saw in him a man of principle who, they believed, would attack with vigor the problems besetting the nation.

Like issue-oriented liberal Democrats or issue-oriented liberal and moderate Republicans, issue-oriented conservative Republicans did not regard politics as a profession. They did not seek political office for the sake of the job or in order to win special privileges but were working for the good society in terms of their interpretation of America's frontier experience and mid-twentieth-century reality. Unlike the other factions of their party, they were extremely unhappy with current trends. They saw America departing radically from its traditional past, and their intense desire to halt the changes lent their work an urgency that was lacking in the efforts of competing groups. As these active conservatives have grown to represent a greater and greater threat to the status quo, the satisfied issue-oriented moderates have been compelled to increase their own activity substantially.

IMPACT ON AMERICAN POLITICS

The immediate impact of the 1964 presidential election on American politics is apparent. It drew into politics large numbers of issue-oriented conservatives who, unlike the issue-oriented Republican moderates or Democratic liberals, are intensely dissatisfied with the content as well as the trends of mid-twentieth-century American life and culture. The conservatives condemn with equal vigor the efforts of Democratic liberals to construct an equalitarian welfare state and the governmental means selected by Republican moderates to attain a frontier-like society. The gulf between the two groups of Republicans does not appear to be insurmountable, however, since they share the same goal and disagree only in their interpretations of the reality of mid-twentieth-century American life. Their differences should be resolved as experience proves whether or not frontier-like opportunities can exist independent of governmental programs designed to provide them.

The long-run consequences of the 1964 election will probably include an acceleration of the process by which the American political parties become more issue-oriented and nationally oriented. As pointed out in Chapter Six, the events of the 1964 Republican convention were both a herald and a precipitant of the weakening of the federal system, despite the homage paid to states' rights. Goldwater's defeat was accompanied by the election of an overwhelmingly Democratic Congress, which promptly enacted into law measures such as medicare and federal aid to education that had long been regarded as responsibilities of state and local governments.

However, those who forecast permanent Republican eclipse are misreading political history and contemporary political trends. A particularly instructive example of the capacity of the Republican party to recover from overwhelming defeat at the polls is provided by the course of events in Ohio following the 1958 election discussed earlier in this chapter. With a view toward destroying the party's identification with the unpopular "right-to-work" measure, pragmatic state chairman Ray Bliss picked up the electoral pieces and returned to his long-time job of attempting to identify the Ohio Republican party with the status quo, including the New Deal measures that provided social justice and more equal opportunities for the disadvantaged. In 1962 this middle-of-the-road Republican party returned to power with even larger margins than those enjoyed by the Democrats in 1958, and it is a relatively safe bet that in 1966 and 1968 the Republican party, led by Bliss as Republican National Chairman, will recapture the loyalty of millions of middle-of-the-road Americans who in 1964 voted for Johnson as the only alternative to Goldwater. The Bliss formula for political success, if followed nationally, might even enable the Republican party to reassume its position as the nation's majority party, for the experience of issue-oriented liberal and moderate Republicans in the nation's industrial states, as exemplified by Lindsay in New York, Romney in Michigan, and Scranton in Pennsylvania, has proved that Democratic opponents can be soundly defeated.

POLITICAL TRENDS IN THE MIDWEST

The observation that the Republican party may regain its pre-1932 position of political pre-eminence as the nation's majority party would seem to fly in the face of facts. The statistics that induced near-despair in the ranks of Republican partisans following the 1964 election were that, besides the President, 33 of the nation's 50 governors, 68 of the 100 senators, and 295 of the 435 representatives were Democrats. But despite this Democratic dominance, election statistics indicate also that the trend in many big industrial states is toward ever larger Republican voting percentages in statewide elections.

ILLINOIS

Illinois provides a suggestive case study of the direction of political movement nationally. Situated at the heart of the country both geographically and culturally, the state in many respects represents the nation in microcosm. Two dominant facts emerge from an analysis of Illinois politics. First, the Democratic party has been flooded by the disinherited of the New Deal period, who flowed into the party as a result of Franklin Roosevelt's policies. As a comparison of Figures 5 and 6 shows, most of the counties in which the Democratic party enjoyed appreciable percentage gains in presidential elections from 1920 to 1960 are also the counties that contained the largest proportion of foreign-born or first-generation residents. Second, the counties in which Democrats fared least well in presidential elections were those that contained the largest proportion of native-born citizens. By and large, many of the foreign-born are East Europeans and Italians living in the larger cities, such as Chicago.[4] They suffered most from the Great Depression and consequently reacted with the greatest gratitude to the relief measures of the New Deal. Their gratitude was translated into Democratic votes in 1936, and they largely remained loyal to the Democrats in elections through 1964.

The Democratic majorities that helped elect Presidents and that elected Democratic congressmen and governors during those years resulted in large part from the marriage within the Democratic party between the disinherited of the Depression generation and the disinherited of earlier generations, who were primarily the grandchildren of people who sympathized with the South during the Civil War. Figure 7 identifies the counties in

Figure 5
Percentage Changes in Illinois Democratic Vote in Presidential Elections,
1920–1960

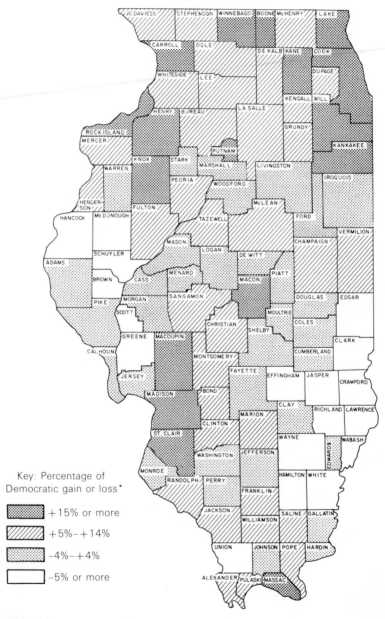

Key: Percentage of
Democratic gain or loss*

+15% or more

+5%–+14%

-4%–+4%

-5% or more

*Political change was measured along a line of regression for each county, and the percentage of change
was the difference between the bottom and the top of the line. Therefore, the amount of change for
each county is a product of all the elections in the time period, not of just the first and last elections.

Figure 6
Percentage of Foreign-Born or First-Generation Residents
in Illinois Counties, 1960

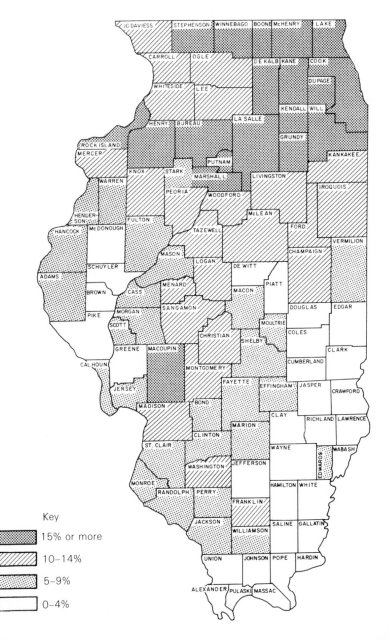

Key

15% or more

10–14%

5–9%

0–4%

Figure 7
Illinois Counties that Supported Democratic or Republican Candidates in All Presidential Elections, 1860–1892

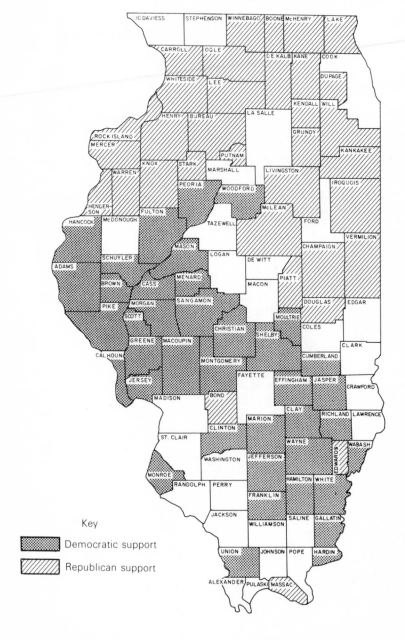

Key

Democratic support

Republican support

Figure 8
Support of Illinois Counties for Democratic or Republican Candidates
in Eight Presidential Elections, 1932–1960

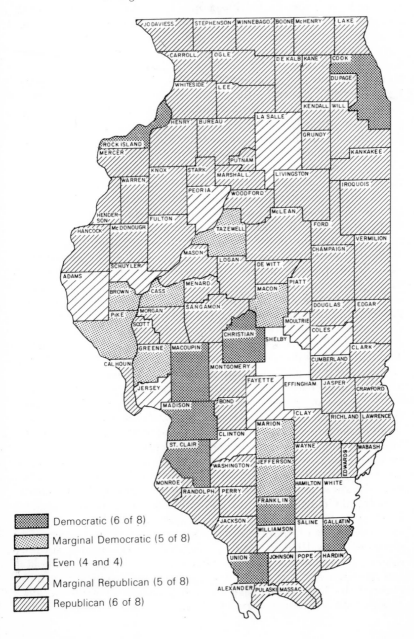

Democratic (6 of 8)

Marginal Democratic (5 of 8)

Even (4 and 4)

Marginal Republican (5 of 8)

Republican (6 of 8)

which a majority of voters consistently supported Democratic presidential candidates after the Civil War, from 1860 through 1892. Those counties, mainly in the southern part of the state, were in most cases settled by people from the South who were antipathetic to the Union cause and who in some instances joined Copperhead (or antiwar) movements. Figure 8 shows that the most Democratic Illinois counties in the presidential elections from 1932 through 1960 were by and large the same southern Illinois counties that traditionally voted Democratic in the nineteenth century, joined by the state's great metropolitan counties — Cook County (Chicago), Rock Island County, and St. Clair County (East St. Louis). Thus, after 1860, the Civil War-generated two-party division in Illinois continued into the New Deal period, with the sections that voted against Lincoln in 1860 and 1864 voting for Franklin Roosevelt, and the sections that supported the Union in the 1860's casting their ballots for Herbert Hoover in 1932.

Another important part of the traditional Democratic vote in Illinois was the German and Irish Catholic vote, which was rooted in the pre-Civil War Know-Nothing period, when the Democratic party was the alternative to an anti-Catholic, anti-foreign vote. Similarly, the Democratic party in Illinois and in the rest of the nation as well was a political counterpoint to the Republican party, which was the political home of the native Protestants who had arrived in America first and who consequently possessed the New World's best land and dominated its goods and opportunities.

Between 1936 and 1960, however, the traditional Democratic voters tended to take leave of the New Deal Democratic party. The native white Protestant Democrats in Illinois had traditionally rationalized their affiliation with that party in terms of its attention to the common man. To these traditional Protestant Democrats whose party allegiance emerged out of the events of the Civil War, after 1932 the party seemed less and less the party of the common man and increasingly the party of metropolitan residents. Moreover, the party seemed to be dominated by elements to which they were at best indifferent and at worst actively antagonistic — the foreign-born, Negroes, and Catholics. Table XII statistically supports these impressionistic statements concerning the direction of political change in Illinois and the character of the two parties. It is evident from the simple coefficients of correlation between the percentage of change in the Democratic vote in presidential elections from 1920 to 1960, on the one hand, and the several demographic and political variables, on the other, that Catholic, foreign-born and first-generation, urban, and nonwhite citizens entered the Democratic party in large numbers over the period. It is equally evident that non-Catholic, native-born, rural, white,

TABLE XII

Correlation Between Percentage of Change in the Democratic Vote in Illinois in Presidential Elections, 1920–1960, and Demographic and Political Variables

	Per cent Catholic residents, 1957[b]	Per cent foreign and first-generation residents, 1960[c]	Per cent rural-farm residents, 1960[c]	Per cent urban residents, 1960[c]	Per cent nonwhite residents, 1960[c]	Per cent Democratic vote, 1860[d]
Percentage of change in Democratic vote in presidential elections, 1920–1960[a]	0.32	0.65	(–)0.62	0.52	0.36	(–)0.40

[a]Political change was measured along a line of regression for each county, and the percentage of change was the difference between the bottom and the top of the line. Therefore, the amount of change for each county was a product of every election in the time period, not of just the first and last elections.

[b]National Council of Churches of Christ, *Churches and Church Membership in the United States,* Series A–E (New York: National Council of Churches, 1956).

[c]U.S. Bureau of the Census. *County and City Data Book, 1962.*

[d]Per cent of total Democratic and Republican vote, excluding votes cast for minor-party candidates. Percentages computed from statistics in Walter D. Burnham. *Presidential Ballots, 1836–1892* (Baltimore: Johns Hopkins University Press, 1955).

and traditionally Democratic residents tended to depart from the Democratic ranks.

Another aspect of the change is that much of Illinois' German and Irish Catholic community, which had previously comprised the "foreign" element of the population, was integrating into the greater community at the same time that East European Catholics entered the party. Due to their becoming part of the "have" as opposed to the "have not" vote, the German and Irish Catholics increasingly adopted the same political prejudices as those held by the white Anglo-Saxon Protestants. They felt as threatened by the newly arrived immigrants and by the white and Negro South as did the native white Protestants — perhaps more so, since their economic status was less firmly established.

This changing political attitude was reflected in Illinois' changing voting patterns. In 1940, 1944, 1948, and 1960, the Democratic margin in Chicago was large enough to carry the state for the Democratic presidential candidate. However, because of the ever-widening Republican margins from downstate Illinois and suburban Cook County, the statewide Democratic margins narrowed almost to the vanishing point and did vanish in 1952 and 1956 when Eisenhower carried the state. In 1960 Kennedy won Chicago by 456,312 votes, a margin exceeded only by Franklin Roosevelt's 1936 plurality of 555,492 votes. But Kennedy won the state by only 8,858 votes compared to Roosevelt's statewide margin of 714,606 votes. The fact that a Catholic headed the Democratic ticket affected the 1960 results, since downstate Illinois is predominantly Protestant, but the trend toward increased Republican pluralities outside Cook County was evident in other elections, with the exception of the 1964 presidential election.

MEDIUM-SIZED CITIES IN MICHIGAN

The trend toward Democratic success in large cities and wherever there are large concentrations of immigrants, and toward Democratic failure in smaller towns with predominantly native white populations, is apparent also in the nation's medium-sized cities, where native whites tend to settle when they move from the country. In Michigan, for example, as shown in Figure 9, Democratic gubernatorial candidate G. Mennen Williams' 1948 statewide electoral margin of 160,000 votes was possible because the sizable Democratic pluralities of 240,000 votes in Wayne County (Detroit) and 35,000 votes in the state's other metropolitan counties were more than sufficient to overcome the Republican pluralities in the less populous counties. After 1948 the Democratic margin in Wayne County increased, but in the other metropolitan counties

Figure 9

Party Pluralities in Michigan Gubernatorial Elections, 1948–1962

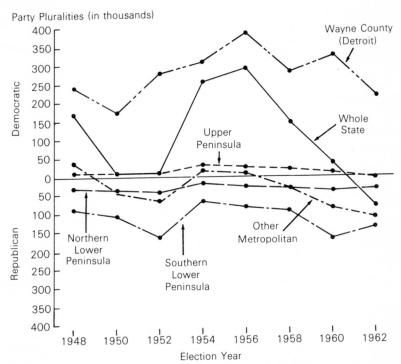

Party Pluralities (in thousands)

SOURCE: John H. Fenton, *Midwest Politics* (New York: Holt, Rinehart & Winston, Inc., 1966), p. 29.

it declined, until in 1962 the metropolitan counties other than
Wayne gave Republican George Romney a plurality of 120,000
votes over his Democratic opponent. The 1962 Wayne County
Democratic plurality of 215,000 remained substantial, but it did
not outweigh the newly Republican vote of the smaller cities plus
the traditionally Republican vote of the less populous sections.

OHIO AND THE CORN BELT

Ohio provides another instructive example of the direction
of voting trends in the 1960's and insights into the reasons behind
them. Figure 10 shows that Democratic pluralities in Ohio's
metropolitan counties registered a steady secular decline between
1936 and 1960 and that Republican pluralities increased almost
as consistently in nonmetropolitan counties. Figure 11 reveals
that the Democratic losses over most of the period were par-

Figure 10
Party Pluralities in Ohio Metropolitan and Nonmetropolitan Counties
in Presidential Elections, 1932–1960

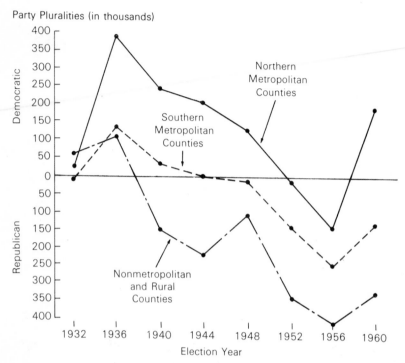

ticularly substantial in the traditionally Democratic corn belt, which in 1932 provided Franklin Roosevelt with the largest part of his plurality in Ohio.

The erosion of native white Democratic strength is particularly apparent in and adjacent to the Midwest corn belt. In Ohio before 1932 the corn belt contained many Democratic voters; in that year, for example, the state's nonmetropolitan counties gave Roosevelt a larger plurality than did the rest of the state (see Figure 10). In 1936, however, the Democratic vote declined all across the corn belt while it increased elsewhere, due to the fact that corn belt farmers and city people suffered less from the Great Depression than did the residents of less fertile farm areas and less industrially diversified cities. The relative prosperity of the corn belt farm areas had its impact on business activity in the adjoining cities, and the industries associated with food production did not experience as much unemployment as did the hard goods and mass-production industries. Thus, such corn belt cities as Cincinnati, Columbus, and Indianapolis are presently regarded

Figure 11
Party Pluralities in Ohio Corn Belt and Other Counties
in Presidential Elections, 1932–1960

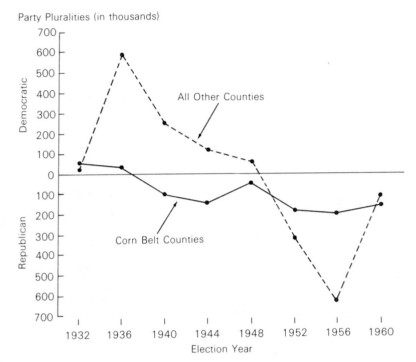

as largely Republican cities; they differ from such Democratic-inclined cities as Cleveland, Detroit, and Chicago primarily in their relatively small foreign-born and second-generation populations.[5]

The Democratic victory in 1960, then, was won by reactivating the coalition of Civil War and Depression disinherited. Catholic voters were temporarily recaptured through the nomination of a Catholic candidate for President, while the loyalty of some traditional white Protestant Democrats was retained through the device of nominating a Protestant for the vice-presidency. The 1960 presidential election was a "sport" (in the biological sense) in the history of American politics. It was peculiar because of the Catholic issue; but since the successful Catholic candidate did not hand the keys of the White House to the Pope, the religious issue should never be a major one again.

The 1964 election should mark the end of debate over another old issue. Goldwater revived the economic issues of the New Deal (such as social security and medicare) and thereby temporarily restored the cohesive force of the New Deal coalition, resulting in a disastrous Republican defeat, as Bliss and other moderate Republicans had predicted. The post-1964 success of the Republican party therefore depends in large part on the ability of Republican moderates to persuade their fellows to accept those issues as facts and to retire them from politics. Certainly the 1964 election results provide conclusive arguments in favor of doing so.

The foregoing examples illustrate one important key to the Republican trend that is evident throughout the industrial Midwest. The Italians, Eastern Europeans, Negroes, and other recently arrived groups of people in the cities vote Democratic because of the greater suffering they experienced during and after the Great Depression. The native whites in the corn belt and the cities of the corn belt did not suffer nearly so intensely from the events of the 1930's, and, in addition, they enjoyed almost uninterrupted prosperity from World War II through 1965. Therefore, memories of the Great Depression are dim among those old enough to remember it, and all but nonexistent among those born after 1940. Another conservative influence on native whites is their attitude toward some minority groups, which, they fear, seek a share of their goods and of their job and educational opportunities; this group votes for extremely conservative candidates. However, the election defeats of most such candidates outside the South would indicate that fear of immigrant and Negro groups is not a dominant factor in determining voting behavior. More typically, native white non-Southerners recognize the need of Negroes and others for improved educational and economic opportunities. However, they widely believe that these groups must make their way through individual effort and that government should not force integration and a more equal distribution of economic goods and opportunities through such measures as preferential hiring of Negroes. This belief leads many voters toward the moderate Republican position, which insists on eventual integration and supports measures designed to improve the opportunities available to Negroes but which specifically rejects governmental or extragovernmental efforts to handicap the native white front-runners in the race for the good things of life.

POLITICAL TRENDS IN THE CITIES

When these voting divisions and voting trends in the Midwest are superimposed on the immigration laws enacted in the 1920's, which shut off large-scale emigration from Eastern Europe to the United States, the almost inevitable result is a Republican trend except in areas settled by substantial numbers of Negroes.[6] And when the fact that the more Republican-inclined, medium-sized cities are growing at a more rapid rate than larger metropolitan areas is added to the above, the reasons for pro-Republican trends become even more evident. The newcomers to the medium-sized cities tend to be native whites from surrounding rural areas, and, therefore, they often derive from Republican families. But most important, labor unions are less powerful politically in medium-sized cities than in metropolitan areas, due primarily to their relatively small size and limited resources. In addition, since most Midwestern medium-sized cities have a large number of diversified industries, and consequently a great many trade and industrial unions, no single union is able to dominate the labor movement. Each labor leader jealously guards his narrow area of power and prefers the role of general in a small labor army to that of lieutenant in a mighty unified labor movement. Each leader works out his own political arrangements with candidates, and these are generally oriented toward narrow bread-and-butter objectives.

Partially because of the weakness of labor unions, partially because of the rural conservative backgrounds of much of the labor force, and partially because of residential patterns, working people tend to be much less cohesive in medium-sized cities than in metropolitan areas. In Detroit or Cleveland, a conservative rural Republican who takes a job with the Ford Motor Company or Republic Steel soon learns that he must choose between his Republican voting habits and acceptance in his work group. Whenever he eats, goes bowling, or drinks a beer with his fellow workers, he hears that the Democratic party is the party of the common man and that the Republican party is the party of depression and unemployment. Further, because his neighbors' place of employment and working-class status is probably identical with his own, he tends to carry on the same kinds of conversation at home that he does in the steel mill or auto plant. In medium-sized cities, on the other hand, pressures on a laborer to conform to the voting habits of his working-class fellows are not nearly so intense. His neighbors might well be white-collar Republican voters, with whom he is as likely to bowl and drink beer as with his fellow workers. Most often his social companions will include members of several economic classes, and in his conversations he will therefore be exposed to as many arguments for a Republican vote as for a Democratic vote. Thus he will often maintain any Republican affiliation he may have had when he moved to the city.

POLITICAL TRENDS IN THE NATION

It is probably safe to say that the above conclusions and generalizations concerning political trends in the Midwest apply, with suitable modifications, to Southern, Eastern, and Western politics. In the South, it is apparent that the improved Republican position contains a larger component of fear of and reaction against Negro gains than is true in the Midwest. In the West, the proximity of the frontier in terms of time and geography makes the individualistic arguments of the conservatives more plausible than in the rest of the nation; however, the frontier experience has also left fresher memories of the need for cooperative efforts to cope with problems ranging from Indians to irrigation. The somewhat larger proportions of immigrants residing in the East, and the problems arising from the growth of great metropolitan complexes and the migrations from cities into suburbs, raise questions concerning political trends in that section of the nation that do not exist in the same magnitude elsewhere. Further, the weakening of Republican strength in northern New England would appear to herald the development of new cleavages between the two parties along issue lines rather than the old religious, ethnic, and place-of-residence political divisions.

Nevertheless, judging by the evidence presented here, the present Democratic majority, despite its extraordinary victory in 1964, is most insecure. The only support that appears to be "safe" is that from people who live in cultural ghettoes either by choice or by necessity; but the Harlem vote received by John Lindsay in the 1965 New York City mayorality election would indicate that even this kind of support is not entirely secure. Throughout the nation, the largest part of the "safe" Democratic vote is cast by immigrant and minority-group residents of the metropolitan centers, who identify with the political party that has traditionally been the refuge of the disinherited but who, as we have seen, are being gradually assimilated by the dominant middle-class elements of the population. Obviously, this leaves the Democratic party peculiarly vulnerable.

In many ways this present Democratic party support resembles the support it received during the last half of the nineteenth century from elements outside the main thrust of American society. After 1860 the party's votes came from people unhappy with the results of the Civil War and after 1896 from those discontented with the effects of the Industrial Revolution. True enough, millions of middle-class Americans voted for Democratic candidates in 1964 because in that election only the Democrats promised to make active attacks on problems such as education, medical care for the aged, river pollution, and social welfare. Few of the new elements moving into the Republican party wanted to return to the pre-New Deal America that Goldwater seemed to wish to recapture. The newly Republican Irish and Germans who had moved from slums to middle-class neighborhoods associated pre-New Deal days with poverty and insecurity. Similarly, the farmers' sons who were working in the cities and voting Republican had a stake in the status quo through social security, unemployment compensation, and seniority rights, which are protected by contracts between unions and management.

These people are conservative in the truest sense of the word. They are generally content with things as they are, and while they do not generally oppose measures providing improved opportunities for the underprivileged, they strongly oppose radical proposals that threaten to hinder their own progress or, worse, to plunge them back into the slums or to the marginal farms from which they have so recently escaped. Hence their Democratic votes in 1964 in opposition to right-wing extremism. However, when moderate or liberal Republicans retired the New Deal from politics by persuading people that they accepted social security and unions, these same voters rushed to support the party that emphasized opportunities and social justice. They increasingly vote Republican when offered a moderate Republican candidate who promises to administer the status quo in the most effective and efficient manner possible. As Arthur Schlesinger, Sr., has pointed out, the nation has a long history of cycles of reform and consolidation.[7] In the mid-twentieth century the Democratic party is the party of reform, and people turn to the Republicans when they tire of reform and want new programs to be better managed.

The result of the right-to-work balloting in Ohio in 1958, described earlier, was a testimonial to this commitment of conservative Americans to the status quo. Ohio Republican leaders were opposed to both the right-to-work proposal and Goldwater's candidacy as tending to reawaken memories of the 1930's. They recognized that a victorious Republican party is a coalition of pre-1932 voters with people who have prospered since the New Deal and that an extremist candidate automatically sacrifices the second part of this coalition to the Democratic party.

Paradoxically, then, the development of more issue-oriented and nationally oriented parties should work to the long-run advantage of the Republican party, provided it hews to the middle of the political road. This does not contradict the earlier evidence of a positive relationship between issue-oriented politics and governmental programs designed to reallocate goods and oppor-

tunities. Such programs should continue to expand under Republican rule and Democratic goading, as indeed they have in
Michigan and New York. The ranks of the disinherited are
declining; the old coalition of the Southern disinherited and
the disinherited ethnic groups of the North is forever shattered,
and the trickle of immigrants entering the United States provides
few fresh battalions of hungry and bewildered people to replace
the Irish and Italians and Polish of yesteryear.

Thus, in issue-oriented politics at the national level, middle-
class Americans interested in maintaining the status quo should
once again be in a numerical position to seat themselves in the
saddle of power. Their policy predilections apparently appeal to
the economic and psychic self-interest of a majority of the population. This could be a healthy national development if middle-class
Americans reach out to assimilate and integrate the undigested
groups that remain in American society, thus binding more
closely together the North and the South, Catholics and Protestants, white and black, privileged and underprivileged. From
such national alliances should develop a more widely held American community of feeling, induced by more frequent interaction
on the basis of common interests and producing attitudes of
empathy and sympathy among fellow Americans.

FOOTNOTES

CHAPTER ONE

1. See W. E. Binkley, *American Political Parties*, 4th ed. (New York: Alfred A. Knopf, Inc., 1963), and James M. Burns, *The Deadlock of Democracy* (Englewood Cliffs, N.J.: Prentice-Hall, Inc., 1963), Chapters 1-8.
2. See R. A. Dahl, *A Preface to Democratic Theory* (Chicago: University of Chicago Press, 1956), and Austin Ranney and Willmoore Kendall, *Democracy and the American Party System* (New York: Harcourt, Brace & Co., 1956).
3. V. O. Key, Jr., *Politics, Parties, and Pressure Groups*, 5th ed. (New York: Thomas Y. Crowell Co., 1964), p. 222.
4. David B. Truman, *The Governmental Process* (New York: Alfred A. Knopf, Inc., 1951), especially Chapters 2-6.
5. See, for example, Pendleton Herring, *The Politics of Democracy* (New York: Rinehart & Company, Inc., 1940).
6. Committee on Political Parties of the American Political Science Association, *Toward a More Responsible Two-Party System* (New York: Holt, Rinehart & Co., 1950), p. v.
7. Willmoore Kendall, "The Two Majorities," *Midwest Journal of Political Science*, IV (1960), 317.
8. Burns, *The Deadlock of Democracy*.
9. James Madison's philosophy of government as presented in *The Federalist* (1789) and as found in the Constitution of the United States represents an attempted compromise between the democratic principle of majority rule and protection of the rights of the minorities within society. Madison refused to rely upon the "good faith" and "Christian charity" of the majority and instead insisted upon a number of institutional checks upon the majority which were incorporated into the Constitution or into custom, such as the presidential veto and judicial review. The basic principle of the Madisonian philosophy was the fragmentation of power in such a way as to make tyranny impossible.
10. See V. O. Key, Jr., *Southern Politics* (New York: Alfred A. Knopf, Inc., 1949); John H. Fenton, *Politics in the Border States* (New Orleans: Hauser Press, 1957) and *Midwest Politics* (New York: Holt, Rinehart & Winston, Inc., 1966); Frank H. Jonas, ed., *Western Politics* (Salt Lake City: University of Utah Press, 1961); Duane Lockard, *New England State Politics* (Princeton, N.J.: Princeton University Press, 1959); and Edward C. Banfield and James Q. Wilson, *City Politics* (Cambridge, Mass.: Harvard University Press and the M.I.T. Press, 1963).
11. The numbers of such studies are legion. Peter H. Odegard's *Pressure Politics: The Story of the Anti-Saloon League* (New York: Columbia University Press, 1928) and Oliver Garceau's *The Political Life of the American Medical Association* (Cambridge, Mass.: Harvard University Press, 1941) treat of formal organization but also deal with the informal side. James M. Burns' *Roosevelt: The Lion and the Fox* (New York: Harcourt, Brace & Co., 1956) is a good example of a political biography, and Theodore H. White's *The Making of the President, 1960* (New York: Atheneum House, Inc., 1961) provides a

useful as well as interesting
account of a political event.
12. See John H. Fenton and
Kenneth Vines, "Negro Registration in Louisiana," *American
Political Science Review,* LI (1957),
704.
13. Angus Campbell *et al., The
American Voter* (New York: John
Wiley & Sons, Inc., 1964).
14. Anthony Downs, *An Eco-
nomic Theory of Democracy* (New
York: Harper & Brothers, 1957).
15. See, for example, White's
The Making of the President, 1960.
16. Theodore Abel, "An Opera-
tion Called Verstehen," in H.
Feigh and M. Brodbeck, eds.,
*Readings in the Philosophy of
Science* (New York: Appleton-
Century-Crofts, Inc., 1953).
17. Floyd Hunter, *Community
Power Structure* (Chapel Hill:
University of North Carolina
Press, 1953).
18. Robert Dahl, *Who Governs?*
(New Haven, Conn.: Yale University Press, 1962).
19. William F. Whyte, *Street
Corner Society* (Chicago: University of Chicago Press, 1943).
CHAPTER TWO
1. V. O. Key, Jr., *Southern
Politics* (New York: Alfred A.
Knopf, Inc., 1949), pp. 298-311.
2. The data in this chapter were
taken from a paper entitled "Two-
Party Competition and Governmental Expenditures" delivered
by the author at the September
1962 meeting of the American
Political Science Association.
3. Efforts to relate welfare
expenditures and two-party
competition include Duane Lockard, *New England State Politics*
(Princeton, N.J.: Princeton University Press, 1959), Chapter
12. A more recent attempt,
published since this study was

written, is Richard E. Dawson
and James A. Robinson, "Inter-
Party Competition, Economic
Variables, and Welfare Policies
in the American States," *Journal
of Politics,* XXV (1963), 265.
Early efforts to measure two-
party competition in the states
include Joseph A. Schlesinger,
"A Two-Dimensional Scheme
for Classifying the States According to Degree of Inter-
Party Competition," *American
Political Science Review,* IL (1955),
1120, and Austin Ranney and
Willmoore Kendall, "The American Party Systems," *American
Political Science Review,* XLVIII
(1954), 477. (See Bibliographical
Essay for a fuller discussion of
these studies.)
4. It is possible that Connecticut's low rank is due to the
high incomes of suburban dwel-
lers near New York City, which
distorts the per capita income
figure for the state.

CHAPTER THREE
1. This account of political
development in Michigan is
drawn from John H. Fenton,
Midwest Politics (New York: Holt,
Rinehart & Winston, Inc., 1966).
Other books that deal with or
provide insight into the origins
and effects of issue-oriented
parties include Leon D. Epstein,
Politics in Wisconsin (Madison:
University of Wisconsin Press,
1958); G. T. Mitau, *Politics in
Minnesota* (Minneapolis: Uni-
versity of Minnesota Press, 1960);
Stephen B. and Vera H. Sarasohn,
*Political Party Patterns in Michi-
gan* (Detroit: Wayne State Uni-
versity Press, 1957); and Robert L.
Sawyer, Jr., *The Democratic State
Central Committee in Michigan* (Ann
Arbor: Institute of Public Ad-

ministration, University of Michigan, 1960).

2. See Sawyer, *The Democratic State Central Committee in Michigan,* p. 29.

3. This observation is largely impressionistic, but any reader who has attended meetings of the John Birch Society or of Goldwater enthusiasts must have noted the presence of large numbers of zealous middle-class women.

4. See Anthony Downs, *An Economic Theory of Democracy* (New York: Harper & Brothers, 1957).

5. See, for example, Edward C. Banfield and James Q. Wilson, *City Politics* (Cambridge, Mass.: Harvard University Press and the M.I.T. Press, 1963).

6. Léon Blum, Socialist statesman who, at the head of France's first Popular Front government in 1936, proposed many socialistic reforms. Conservative opposition to his fiscal measures forced his resignation in 1937.

7. Fenton, *Midwest Politics.*

CHAPTER FOUR

1. This account of Kentucky's job-oriented system is taken from John H. Fenton, *Politics in the Border States* (New Orleans: Hauser Press, 1957).

2. A similar example is provided by Smith Broadbent, Jr., the administration man in Trigg County, who once commented in an interview: "If it were your decision to make, wouldn't you build the road past your friend's house rather than your enemy's?"

3. See Moisei Ostrogorski, *Democracy and the Organization of Political Parties,* Vol. II, *The United States* (Garden City: Doubleday & Company, Inc., 1964), p. 297, on the question of parties as sustainers of old cleavages and

mufflers of new ones. Ostrogorski makes the following observation: "To immobility of political forms in the State the stereotyped party organization tended to add immobility of mind in this political society, where growing wealth increased the number of persons who are satisfied with things as they are. To preserve its cadres, the organization was always trying to make opinion crystallize within them, to prevent the new currents of public feeling from gathering volume and flowing into fresh channels. It kept opinion a prisoner inside old formulas which often were nothing but pure conventions. It veiled or conjured away divergences of views which were making progress in the mind or in the conscience of the nation; and to stop their advance, it did not stick even at fraud or corruption. Party formalism thus puts obstacles in the path of progress and creates dangers to the healthy development of political life, the gravity of which increases in proportion as the nation grows older; it is paving the way for a reaction in an anticonservative direction, of which the politico-social movements in recent years, such as Populism, 'Bryanism,' are warnings resembling the mutterings of the coming storm."

4. Fenton, *Politics in the Border States,* pp. 220-221.

5. *Ibid.,* p. 101.

6. *Ibid.,* pp. 106-107.

CHAPTER FIVE

1. The national scene has usually been characterized by a majority party and a minority party, with the latter always a threat but winning far less than half the elections. However, in the long run the two major parties have enjoyed power for approximately the same periods of time. From 1856 through 1964, the Republicans won sixteen presidential elections and the Democrats twelve.

2. V. O. Key, Jr., *Southern Politics* (New York: Alfred A. Knopf, Inc., 1949), pp. 298-311.

3. See *Ibid.*, pp. 142-150.

4. *Ibid.*, pp. 41, 37-38.

5. Long manufactured interest groups to oppose the dominant business groups through the use of state tax funds. He created business enterprises, established a newspaper, and built a powerful political machine.

CHAPTER SIX

1. The following analysis of the effect of the New Deal and the Great Depression on political attitudes is derived in large part from Richard Judd, *The New Deal in Vermont,* to be published by the Harvard University Press.

2. James M. Burns, *The Deadlock of Democracy* (Englewood Cliffs, N.J.: Prentice-Hall, Inc., 1963).

3. Raymond Wolfinger and Joan Heifetz, "Safe Seats, Seniority, and Power in Congress," *American Political Science Review,* LIX (June 1965), 347.

4. Witness the fight over the seating of the Mississippi delegation at the 1964 convention; it was finally resolved by dividing the seats between the Negro-led Freedom Democrats and the "lily-white" state Democrats.

5. See Wolfinger and Heifetz, "Safe Seats, Seniority, and Power in Congress."

6. *The New York Times,* January 5, 1965, p. 16.

CHAPTER SEVEN

1. See Lawrence H. Fuchs, *The Political Behavior of American Jews* (Glencoe, Ill.: The Free Press, 1956), p. 75.

2. *Ibid.,* pp. 74-76.

3. It should be noted, however, that, similar in many respects to issue-oriented liberal Democrats and moderate Republicans, the upper-middle-class physicians, lawyers, housewives, college professors, and businessmen who comprised the conservative faction often contributed intelligent and devoted service and frequently did an excellent job of organizing their precincts.

4. The largest numbers of the 2,015,562 first- and second-generation residents of Chicago were from Poland (340,144), Germany (293,606), Italy (212,076), Russia (129,349), Ireland (113,622), and Czechoslovakia (108,369). See U.S. Bureau of the Census, *United States Census of Population: 1960,* Vol. I, *Characteristics of the Population,* Part 15, "Illinois" (Washington, D.C.: Government Printing Office, 1963), Table 99.

5. Tables A and B provide data supporting the general statements in the text asserting a positive relationship between percentages of foreign-born and first- and second-generation elements in the populations of large cities and percentage of the vote cast for Democratic candidates.

6. In 1920, foreign-born individuals comprised 13.2 per cent of the total United States population; in 1930, 11.6 per cent; in 1940, 8.8 per cent; in 1950, 6.8 per cent; and in 1960, 5.4 per cent. See U.S. Bureau of the Census, *Historical Statistics of the United States, Colonial Times to 1957* (Washington, D.C.: Govern-

ment Printing Office, 1960), and
U.S. Bureau of the Census,
County and City Data Book, 1962
(Washington, D.C.: Government
Printing Office, 1962).

7. Arthur M. Schlesinger, Sr.,
"Tides of American Politics,"
Yale Review, XXIX (December
1939), 217-230.

TABLE A

Large Cities with High Percentage of Foreign Population

	Total popu-lation, 1960	Per cent foreign, 1960	Per cent Democratic vote*	
			1960	1964
Chicago (Cook County)	5,129,725	34.2	56.5	63.7
Cleveland (Cuyahoga County)	1,647,895	33.5	59.8	71.3
Detroit (Wayne County)	2,666,297	31.2	66.2	76.1

TABLE B

Smaller Cities with Lower Percentage of Foreign Population

	Total popu-lation, 1960	Per cent foreign, 1960	Per cent Democratic vote*	
			1960	1964
Columbus (Franklin County)	682,962	8.7	40.6	54.1
Cincinnati (Hamilton County)	864,121	11.4	45.5	55.2
Indianapolis (Marion County)	697,567	6.5	42.2	51.6

*Per cent of total Democratic and Republican vote, excluding votes cast for minor-party candidates.
SOURCES: *The World Almanac, 1965* (New York: New York World Telegram and The Sun, 1965); U.S. Bureau of the Census, *County and City Data Book, 1962,* a *Statistical Abstract* supplement, (Washington, D.C. Government Printing Office, 1962).

BIBLIOGRAPHICAL ESSAY

CHAPTER ONE

The reader who desires more extensive treatment of the subject matter in Chapter I should turn to the text by V. O. Key, Jr., *Politics, Parties, and Pressure Groups,* 5th ed. (New York: Thomas Y. Crowell Co., 1964).

An excellent short history of the development of the American two-party system is contained in James M. Burns, *The Deadlock of Democracy* (Englewood Cliffs, N.J.: Prentice-Hall, Inc., 1963), Chapters 1-8. Other useful sources on American party history include W. E. Binkley, *American Political Parties, Their Natural History,* 4th ed. (New York: Alfred A. Knopf, Inc., 1963); C. A. M. Ewing, *Presidential Elections from Abraham Lincoln to Franklin D. Roosevelt* (Norman: University of Oklahoma Press, 1940); Richard Hofstadter, *The American Political Tradition* (New York: Vintage Press, 1954); Malcolm Moos, *The Republicans, A History of Their Party* (New York: Random House, 1956); and E. E. Robinson, *The Evolution of American Political Parties* (New York: Harcourt, Brace & Co., 1924).

Two of the best assessments of the two-party competitive system are Robert A. Dahl, *A Preface to Democratic Theory* (Chicago: University of Chicago Press, 1956) and Austin Ranney and Willmoore Kendall, *Democracy and the American Party System* (New York: Harcourt, Brace & Co., 1956). Other useful and interesting studies include Charles A. Beard, *The American Party Battle* (New York: The Macmillan Co., 1928);

Anthony Downs, *An Economic Theory of Democracy* (New York: Harper & Bros., 1957); Samuel Lubell, *The Future of American Politics* (New York: Harper & Bros., 1952); E. E. Schattschneider, *Party Government* (New York: Farrar and Rinehart, 1942); Theodore H. White, *The Making of the President, 1960* (New York: Atheneum Publishing Co., 1961); Norton Long, "Party Government in the United States," *Journal of Politics,* XIII (May 1951), 187; Donald E. Stokes, "Spatial Models of Party Competition," *American Political Science Review,* LVII (1963), 368; and J. W. Castevens and Charles Press, "Context of Democratic Competition in American State Politics," *American Journal of Science,* LXVIII (1963), 536.

Any student who is seriously interested in the subject of pressure groups must sooner or later (preferably sooner) read David Truman, *The Governmental Process* (New York: Alfred A. Knopf, Inc., 1951). Other studies dealing with the topic both in general and in terms of particular interest groups are legion. Some of the better ones are J. D. Hicks, *The Populist Revolt* (Minneapolis: University of Minnesota Press, 1931); Arthur Kornhauser, *When Labor Votes* (New York: University Books, 1956); Seymour Lipset *et al., Union Democracy* (Glencoe, Ill.: The Free Press, 1956); Grant McConnell, *The Decline of Agrarian Democracy* (Berkeley: University of California Press, 1953); F. W. Riggs, *Pressures on Congress* (New York: King's Crown Press, 1950); E. E. Schattschneider, *Politics, Pressures and the Tariff* (Englewood Cliffs, N.J.: Prentice-Hall,

Inc., 1936); and Gabriel Almond, "A Comparative Study of Interest Groups and the Political Process," *American Political Science Review,* LII (1958), 270.

Some interesting and useful analyses of political party organization are to be found in Hugh A. Bone, *Party Committees and National Politics* (Seattle; University of Washington Press, 1958); H. F. Gosnell, *The American Party System,* 4th ed. (New York: The Macmillan Co., 1949) and *Machine Politics: Chicago Model* (Chicago: University of Chicago Press, 1926); E. Pendleton Herring, *The Politics of Democracy* (Rinehart & Co., 1940); Paul T. David, Ralph M. Goldman, and Richard C. Bain, *The Politics of National Party Conventions* (Washington, D.C.: The Brookings Institution, 1960); and Committee on Political Parties of the APSA, *Toward a More Responsible Two-Party System* (New York: Holt, Rinehart & Co., 1950).

The best recent assessment of the relationships among the political parties, the President, and Congress is to be found in Burns, *The Deadlock of Democracy* (*above*), Chapters 9-14. A good rationale for the preservation of the Madisonian formula for a separation of powers is contained in Willmoore Kendall, "The Two Majorities," *Midwest Journal of Political Science,* IV (1960), 317. Other useful treatments include Wilfred Binkley, *President and Congress* (New York: Alfred A. Knopf, Inc., 1947); James M. Burns, *Roosevelt: the Lion and the Fox* (New York: Harcourt, Brace & Co., 1956); Harold Laski, *The American Presidency* (New York: Harper & Row,

1940); Duncan MacRae, Jr., *Dimensions of Congressional Voting* (Berkeley: University of California Press, 1958); Richard E. Neustadt, *Presidential Power* (New York: John Wiley & Sons, Inc., 1960); David B. Truman, *The Congressional Party* (New York: John Wiley & Sons, Inc., 1959); Richard Neustadt, "Presidency and Legislation: The Growth of Central Clearance," *American Political Science Review,* XLVIII (1954), 641; and Raymond E. Wolfinger and Joan Heifetz, "Safe Seats, Seniority, and Power in Congress," *American Political Science Review,* XLIX (1965), 337.

Important books for the student who is seriously interested in state and city politics are Edward C. Banfield, *Political Influence* (New York: The Free Press, 1961); Edward C. Banfield and James Q. Wilson, *City Politics* (Cambridge, Mass.: Harvard University Press and M.I.T. Press, 1963); John H. Fenton, *Midwest Politics* (New York: Holt, Rinehart and Winston, Inc., 1966) and *Politics in the Border States* (New Orleans: Hauser Press, 1957); Frank H. Jonas, ed., *Western Politics* (Salt Lake City: University of Utah Press, 1961); V. O. Key, Jr., *American State Politics* (New York: Alfred A. Knopf, Inc., 1956) and *Southern Politics* (New York: Alfred A. Knopf, Inc., 1949); Duane Lockard, *New England State Politics* (Princeton, N.J.: Princeton University Press, 1959); and Thomas A. Flinn, "Party Responsibility in the States: Some Causal Factors," *American Political Science Review,* LVIII (1964), 60.

Useful treatments of minor parties include T. H. Greer, *American Social Reform Movements* (Englewood Cliffs, N.J.; Prentice-

Hall, Inc., 1949); W. B. Hesseltine, *The Rise and Fall of Third Parties* (Washington, D.C.: Public Affairs Press, 1948); Irving Howe and Lewis Coser, *The American Communist Party* (Boston: Beacon Press, 1957); H. P. Nash, Jr., *Third Parties in American Politics* (Washington, D.C.: Public Affairs Press, 1959); R. B. Nye, *Midwestern Progressive Politics* (East Lansing: Michigan State College Press, 1951); David J. Saposs, *Communism in American Politics* (Washington, D.C.: Public Affairs Press, 1960); D. A. Shannon, *The Socialist Party of America* (New York: The Macmillan Co., 1955); and M. S. Stedman, Jr., and S. W. Stedman, *Discontent at the Polls, A Study of Farmer and Labor Parties, 1827-1948* (New York: Columbia University Press, 1950).

A good sourcebook for techniques in handling aggregative data is V. O. Key, Jr., *A Primer of Statistics for Political Scientists* (New York: Thomas Y. Crowell Co., 1954). An excellent survey of research methods in public opinion and related research is contained in Bernard Berelson and Morris Janowitz, eds., *Reader in Public Opinion and Communication*, 2nd ed. (New York: The Free Press, 1966).

CHAPTER TWO

There is a growing literature on the relationship between the levels of state government expenditures and political and demographic variables. One of the pioneering attempts to relate political competition and state governmental programs was made by Duane Lockard in *New England State Politics* (Princeton, N.J.: Princeton University Press, 1959), Chapter 12. Earlier efforts

to measure differential levels of two-party competition in the states include Joseph A. Schlesinger, "A Two-Dimensional Scheme for Classifying the States According to Degree of Inter-Party Competition," *American Political Science Review*, IL (1955), 1120, and Austin Ranney and Willmoore Kendall, "The American Party Systems," *American Political Science Review*, XLVIII (1954), 477. More recently, several writers have attempted to use more sophisticated statistical techniques in measuring the relationships between political competition and state governmental programs. An example is the article by Richard E. Dawson and James I. Robinson, "Inter-Party Competition, Economic Variables, and Welfare Policies in the American States," *Journal of Politics*, XXV (1963), 265. Dawson and Robinson's findings with respect to the simple correlations between competition, state expenditures, urbanism, and income were quite similar to my own in Chapter Two. However, Dawson and Robinson failed to separate out the proportionate contribution of competition to multiple relationships between the expenditure variables and the several "external conditions" and competition. Instead, they separated the states into three groups according to income. They then computed simple correlations between competition and state expenditures for the high income, middle income, and low income groups of states. They found little or no relationship between competition and expenditures by this method. They then divided the states into three competitive groupings and related income to state expenditures. They found a fairly close relationship this time. They concluded that the wealth of a state is probably more important than two-party competition in influencing the given state expenditures. The flaws in the methodology are several: 1) It failed in its effort to hold wealth or competition constant, for within each of the divisions of the states it is probable that a relationship between the two variables was present; 2) it is impossible to make statements concerning the relationships between variables for all states on the basis of relationships found for classifications of the states. It would be possible (though unlikely) to arrive at one result for each of the three divisions and arrive at a totally different result for all the states; 3) the measurements tell us nothing at all about the relative contributions of the competition and "external" variables to the variations in expenditures by states.

CHAPTER THREE

Very little has been written on the subject of issue-oriented two-party politics in the United States. Some books dealing with the topic are Fenton, *Midwest Politics* (*above*); Leon D. Epstein, *Politics in Wisconsin* (Madison: University of Wisconsin Press, 1958); G. T. Mitau, *Politics in Minnesota* (Minneapolis: University of Minnesota Press, 1960); Stephen B. and Vera H.Sarasohn, *Political Party Patterns in Michigan* (Detroit: Wayne State University Press, 1957); and Robert L. Sawyer, Jr., *The Democratic State Central Committee in Michigan* (Ann Arbor: Institute of Public Administration, University of Michigan, 1960).

CHAPTER FOUR

There are many books describing traditional job-oriented political organizations. The best descriptive model of the traditional political party is contained in Anthony Downs, *An Economic Theory of Democracy* (*above*). Interesting descriptions of political machines include Gosnell, *Machine Politics: Chicago Model* (*above*); Fenton, *Politics in the Border States* and *Midwest Politics* (*above*); Edwin O'Connor, *The Last Hurrah* (London: Max Reinhardt, 1956); William L. Riordin, *Plunkitt of Tammany Hall* (New York: Alfred A. Knopf, Inc., 1948); and Edward C. Banfield and James Q. Wilson, *City Politics* (*above*).

CHAPTER FIVE

The classic study by V. O. Key, Jr., *Southern Politics*, is required reading for any serious student of American politics. Other useful and interesting treatments of various aspects of one-party politics include A. P. Sindler, *Huey Long's Louisiana* (Baltimore: Johns Hopkins Press, 1956) and Warren E. Miller, "One-Party Politics and the Voter," *American Political Science Review*, L (1956), 707. Some "feel" for the effect of one-party politics on government, and through government on the people, may be obtained from studies of government and administration in Southern states, such as Robert B. Highsaw and C. N. Fortenberry, *The Government and Administration of Mississippi* (New York: Thomas Y. Crowell Co., 1956) and William Goodman, *Inherited Domain: Political Parties in Tennessee* (Knoxville: Bureau of Public Administration, University of Tennessee, 1954).

CHAPTER SIX

The best recent analysis of the American political system is Burns, *The Deadlock of Democracy* (*above*). The descriptions of the 1960 and 1964 presidential campaigns by Theodore H. White, *The Making of the President, 1960* (*above*) and *The Making of the President, 1964* (New York: Atheneum Publishing Co., 1965) provide useful insights into current trends in national two-party politics.

SOURCES OF ELECTION STATISTICS

Presidential election data by states and counties are available for the period 1836-1960 in Walter D. Burnham, *Presidential Ballots, 1836-1892* (Baltimore: Johns Hopkins Press, 1955); Edgar E. Robinson, *The Presidential Vote, 1896-1932* (Stanford, Calif.: Stanford University Press, 1934) and *They Voted for Roosevelt, the Presidential Vote, 1932-1944* (Stanford, Calif.: Stanford University Press, 1947); George Gallup, *The Political Almanac, 1952* (New York: Forbes, 1952), which contains the 1948 election results; and Richard M. Scammon, *America Votes* (Washington, D.C.: Governmental Affairs Institute): Vol. 1 (1952); Vol. 2 (1956); Vol. 3 (1958); Vol. 4 (1960); Vol. 5 (1962). *The World Almanac* for 1965 contains the 1964 presidential election results by states and counties; *The World Almanac* is always one of the first readily available sources of such data.

The student in search of election data other than presidential would be well advised to turn first to the bibliography prepared by Charles Press and Oliver Williams, *State Manuals, Blue Books and Election Results* (Berkeley: Institute of Governmental Studies, University of California, 1962). In most cases, general election and primary election data by counties may be obtained from the office of the secretary of state in individual states. In addition, a number of compilations of individual state election data have been published. See, for example, H. L. Aldefer and R. M. Sigmond, *Presidential Elections by Pennsylvania Counties, 1920-1940* (State College: Pennsylvania State College Studies, No. 10, 1941); H. L. Alderfer and Fannette H. Luhrs, *Gubernatorial Elections in Pennsylvania, 1922-1946* (State College: Pennsylvania Municipal Publications Service, 1946); Oliver Benson, *Oklahoma Votes, 1907-1962* (Norman: Bureau of Government Research, University of Oklahoma, Publication No. 53, 1964); June G. Cabe and Charles A. Sullivan, *Kansas Votes, National Elections, 1859-1956* (Lawrence: Governmental Research Center, University of Kansas, 1957); Alan L. Clem, *Precinct Voting: The Vote in Eastern South Dakota, 1940-1960* (Vermillion: Bureau of Government Research, University of South Dakota, Bureau Report No. 50, 1963) and *West River Voting Patterns: The Vote in Western South Dakota, 1940-1960* (Vermillion: Bureau of Government Research, University of South Dakota, Research Report No. 52, 1965); James R. Donoghue, *How Wisconsin Voted, 1848-1954* (Madison: Bureau of Government, University of Wisconsin Extension Division, 1956); Samuel K. Gove, ed., *Illinois Votes, 1900-1958* (Urbana: Institute of Government and Public Affairs,

University of Illinois, 1959);
Annie Mary Hartsfield, *Florida Votes, 1920-1962* (Tallahassee: Institute of Government Research, Florida State University, Government Series No. 1, 1963); William C. Havard, *et al.*, *Louisiana Elections of 1960* (Baton Rouge: Louisiana State University Press, University Studies, Science Series No. 9, 1963); Alexander Heard and Donald S. Strong, *Southern Primaries and Elections, 1920-1949* (University: University of Alabama Press, 1950); Malcolm E. Jewell, *Kentucky Votes* (Lexington: University of Kentucky Press, 1963), Vols. 1-3; Donald R. Matthews, *North Carolina Votes* (Chapel Hill: University of North Carolina Press, 1963); Robert J. Pitchell, *Indiana Votes* (Bloomington: Bureau of Government Research, Indiana University, 1960); Richard M. Scammon, *Southern Primaries '58* (Washington, D.C.: Governmental Affairs Institute, 1959); Jaspar B. Shannon and Ruth McQuown, *Presidential Politics in Kentucky, 1824-1948* (Lexington: Bureau of Government Research, University of Kentucky, 1950); Texas University Department of Government, *Texas Votes: Selected General and Special Election Statistics, 1944-1963* (Austin: University of Texas, Public Affairs Series No. 59, 1964); Ellis L. Waldron, *Montana Politics Since 1864* (Missoula: Montana State University, 1958); and John P. White, *Michigan Votes: Election Statistics, 1928-1956* (Ann

Arbor: Bureau of Government, Institute of Public Administration, University of Michigan, 1958).

The results of elections for the United States House of Representatives by congressional districts and for the Senate by states may be obtained from the *Congressional Quarterly Almanac* (Washington, D.C.: Congressional Quarterly Service), published annually; *The Congressional Directory* (Washington, D.C.: Government Printing Office), published biannually; Clerk of the House of Representatives, *Statistics of the Congressional Election* (Washington, D.C.: Government Printing Office), published biennially; and U.S. Bureau of the Census, *The Congressional District Data Book* (Washington, D.C.: Government Printing Office, 1963), a supplement to *Statistical Abstract.*

Other miscellaneous collections of election statistics by states and counties include Louis H. Bean, *How to Predict Elections* (New York: Alfred A. Knopf, Inc., 1948), Appendix; Francis Curtis, *The Republican Party, 1854-1904* (New York: G. P. Putnam's Sons, 1904); George Gallup, *The Gallup Political Almanac for 1948* (Princeton, N.J.: American Institute of Public Opinion, 1948) and *The Political Almanac with 1953 Supplement* (New York: Forbes, 1953); and U. S. Bureau of the Census, *Vote Cast in Presidential and Congressional Elections, 1928-1944* (Washington, D.C.: Government Printing Office, 1946).

INDEX

A

Abel, Theodore, 28
Affiliation, party, factors in, 4-10
Age of Jackson, 4-5
Aggregative approach to the study of political parties, 23-24
Agricultural Adjustment Act, 7
Alabama, one-party politics in, 82, 84-85
American Political Science Association, 18
American Voter, The, 27
Americans for Democratic Action, 55, 114
Anecdotal approach to the study of political parties, 23-24

B

Barefoot empiricism, 22, 24
Barkley, Alben, 9
Behavioralism, 22, 27
Bifactional one-party politics, 85-87
Bilbo, Theodore G., 20
Blatnik, John A., 102
Bliss, Ray, 112, 116, 128
Blizzard, Bill, 73, 74
Bricker, John, 72
British politics: influence of, 2-3; organization of, 92-93; public opinion and, 60-61
Bryan, William Jennings, 6, 8, 21
Burns, James M., 19, 20, 99
Burr, Aaron, 2
Businessmen in politics, 52, 56-57, 61, 63
Byrd, Harry F., 86

C

Chandler, "Happy," 68, 71, 72
Cincinnati, issue-oriented politics in, 97-98
City politics: national politics and, 20; trends in, 128-129
Civil rights: in 1948 election, 8-9; party affiliation and, 71, 128, 130
Civil service laws, 55, 91, 93, 106
Civil War: party affiliation and, 5, 6, 9, 50-51, 71, 72, 117, 122, 127, 130; economics and, 8; one-party politics and, 78, 80-81; orientation and, 48-49
Civilian Conservation Corps, 96
Clark, Joseph, 101
Clements, Earl, iv, v, 67, 69

Combs, Bert T., 67
Committee on Political Parties, 18
Community vs. isolation, 108-110
Community Power Structure, 28
Congress of Industrial Organizations, 54, 55
Congress, parties and, 19-20, 98-103, 105
Conservatives, 111-115, 131
Conventions, national: of 1948, 8-9; of 1952, 111; of 1964, 110-111; organization of, 18, 93
Coolidge, Calvin, 21
Copperheads, 5, 71, 81, 122
Correlations, computation of, 41-42

D

Dahl, Robert, 29
Davis, John W., 21
Deadlock of Democracy, The, 19, 99
De Gaulle, Charles, 61
Democratic party: future of, 130-132; in Illinois, 117-124; in Michigan, 54-57, 59, 124-125; nationalization of, 91-92, 97-103; in Ohio, 125-128; one-party politics and, 81; support of, 4-10, 130-131
Dewey, Thomas E., 8, 9, 12
Dixiecrat party, 9, 21
Downs, Anthony, 27-28

E

Eastland, James, 51
Economic Theory of Democracy, An, 27
Education expenditures and state politics, 33, 35-49
Eisenhower, Dwight D., 9, 12, 111
Election, national presidential: of 1896, 6; of 1936, 7-8, 53; of 1948, 8-9; of 1960, 127; of 1964, 110-117

F

Fair Labor Standards Act, 7
Farmers, Great Depression and, 94-95
Faubus, Orville, 83
Folsom, "Kissin'" Jim, 85
France, politics in, 61
Frontier experience, 3, 112, 114
Future trends, political: in cities, 128-129; in Midwest, 117-128; in nation, 130-132

G

Galbraith, John, 46
Gilligan, John J., 98

Goldwater, Barry, 5, 9, 11, 12, 21, 51, 61, 91, 102, 110, 111, 113, 115, 116, 127, 131
Gompers, Samuel, 67
Government performance: competition and, 35-49; issue-oriented politics and, 64-65, 106; job-oriented politics and, 75-77; one-party politics and, 87-89. *See also* Congress, President.
Governmental Process, The, 14
Great Depression: party affiliation and, 71, 117, 126, 127, 128; nationalization and, 94-96, 106; two-party system and, 7, 78-79

H
Hallanan, Walter, 74
Hamilton, Alexander, 2
Hart, Phil, 101
Heifetz, Joan, 102
Home Owners Loan Corporation, 7
Hoover, Herbert, 7, 62, 122
Humphrey, Hubert, 51, 101
Hunter, Floyd, 28

I
Illinois, political trends in, 117-124
Immigrants, 81-82, 117, 122, 124, 128-129
Interest groups, 13-15; issue-oriented parties and, 63-64; job-oriented parties and, 66-67, 73-75; nationalization and, 97-98; one-party politics and, 84-85, 86-87
Isolation vs. community, 108-110
Issue-oriented politics, 46-49; characteristics of, 57-59; Democratic, 97-99, 101-102; emergence of, 50-57; government performance and, 64-65; interest groups and, 63; nationalization and, 93-97; organization and, 15-16; public opinion and, 59-63; Republican, 91

J
Jackson, Andrew, 3, 4, 8
Jefferson, Thomas, 2, 3
Jews, community feeling of, 109-110
Job-oriented politics, 51; government performance and, 75-77; interest groups and, 66-67, 73-75; in Kentucky, 67-70; organization and, 15-16; public opinion and, 70-73
John Birch Society, 61, 113
Johnson, Lyndon B., 9, 20, 99, 103, 104, 106, 107, 114

K
Kaplan, Robert, 97
Kendall, Willmoore, 19, 20
Kennedy, John F., 92, 99, 106, 114
Kentucky, job-oriented politics in, 67-70, 72
Key, V. O., 12, 22, 32, 80, 82
Know-Nothing party, 122

L
Labor, in politics, 7, 14-15, 52, 55-57, 61, 63, 73-74, 129
La Follette, Robert, 21
Landon, Alfred M., 8, 99
Leadership of parties, 10-13
League of Women Voters, 54
Lincoln, Abraham, 5, 122
Lindsay, John, 116, 130
Local politics, 20. *See also* City politics, State politics.
Long, Earl, 84
Long, Huey, 86

M
McKinley, William, 6, 8, 21
Michigan: political transformation in, 52-57, 59, 63; political trends in, 124-125
Michigan Declaration, 59
Midwest, political trends in, 117-128
Minor parties, 20-22
Model building approach to the study of political parties, 27-28
Multifactional politics, 82-85
Murphy, Frank, 54

N
National Industrial Recovery Act, 96
National Labor Relations Act, 7, 15, 54, 95
National parties: competition between, 10-13; future of, 130-132; history of, 2-10; nationalization of, 93-107; organization of, 15-19, 92-93; strength of, 90-92
National Recovery Act, 54
National Youth Administration, 96
Neely, Matthew M., 73
Negroes: party affiliation of, 4, 5, 8, 122, 129; isolation of, 110; Southern politics and, 80, 84. *See also* Civil rights.
New Deal, 7-8, 12, 94-96, 127-128, 131
Nixon, Richard, 12
Nonpartisan League, 86

O

Ohio, political trends in, 112, 116, 125-128
One-party politics, 32, 48-49, 62; bi-factional, 85-87; causes of, 80-82; characteristics of, 78-80; government performance and, 87-89; interest groups and, 84-85, 86-87; multi-factional, 82-85; public opinion and, 83-84, 86-87
"Operation Called Verstehen, An," 28
Organization, party: issue- vs. job-oriented, 15-19; national, 92-93; recommendations for, 17-19
Orientation: of congressmen, 99-102; of parties, 46-49. *See also* Issue-oriented politics, Job-oriented politics.
Origins of two-party system, 2-4

P

Paine, Thomas, 3
Participant-observation approach to the study of political parties, 28
Political parties, approaches to the study of, 22-29
Politics in the Border States, 71
Populist party, 21, 80
President: nationalization and, 103-105; parties and, 19-20
Pressure groups. *See* Interest groups.
Progressive party, 21
Public opinion: issue-oriented politics and, 59-63; job-oriented politics and, 70-73; one-party politics and, 83-84, 86-87
Public Works Administration, 7, 96

R

Reapportionment, 19, 20
Republican party: in cities, 128-129; future of, 116-117, 131-132; issue-orientation in, 91, 98, 103; in Michigan, 59; in Midwest, 125-128; 1964 presidential campaign and, 110-117; one-party politics and, 80; support of 4-10, 131
Reuther, Walter, 55, 56
Rockefeller, Nelson, 91, 110, 111
Romney, George, 12, 52, 56, 61, 91, 111, 116, 125
Roosevelt, Franklin D., 7, 21, 53, 54, 73, 96, 99, 100, 104, 122, 126
Roosevelt, Theodore, 21

S

Sample survey approach to the study of political parties, 24-27
Schlesinger, Arthur, Sr., 131
Scranton, William, 12, 91, 110, 111, 113, 116
Securities Act, 7
Simpson, Bill, 67, 68, 69, 70
Social Security Act, 7
South, the: congressmen from, 102; one-party politics in, 79-80; 82-89; political trends in, 130
Southern Politics, 22, 32, 80
Staebler, Neil, 52, 55, 102
State politics: competition in, 33-49; government performance and, 35-49; issue-oriented, 64-65, 75-77, 106-107; job-oriented, 70-77; national politics and, 20; types of, 31-35
Stevenson, Adlai, 92, 111, 115
Street Corner Society, 29

T

Taft, Robert, Jr., 98
Taft, William Howard, 21, 111
Tennessee Valley Authority, 7, 79
Thurmond, Strom, 8, 9, 102
Tillman, "Pitchfork Ben," 80
Traditional approach to the study of political parties, 22-23, 28
Truman, David, 14
Truman, Harry S., 8, 9, 21
"The Two Majorities," 19

U

United Auto Workers, 63, 114
United Mine Workers, 73-74
Urbanism: job-oriented politics and, 71-72; state expenditures and, 37-45

W

Wallace, George, 84
Wallace, Henry A., 8, 55
Watson, Albert, 102
Wealth, state expenditures and, 37-45
Welfare expenditures and state politics, 33, 35-49
West Virginia, job-oriented politics in, 73-74
Who Governs? 29
Whyte, William F., 29
Williams, G. Mennen ("Soapy"), 52, 55, 124
Williams, John Bell, 102
Willkie, Wendell, 12

Wilson, Harold, 93
Wilson, Woodrow, 6, 8, 21
Wolfinger, Raymond, 102
Women, in politics, 58-59

Works Progress Administration, 7, 96
World War II, party nationalization
    and, 78-79, 96-97, 106
Wright, Fielding, 9